Having Fun With God

Suzette Lambert, LMFT

DEDICATION

First and foremost this book is dedicated to The King and Kingdom advancement for His Great Name sake, and His Glory. Without Your great hand in my life, Lord, I would truly be lost. I needed Your love, I have always needed Your love.

This book is also dedicated to a man that lived in a house with a bunch of women he called family. He raised us girls in a way that continually showed a passion for God. Not an easy feat, I am sure, but he was persistent. My dad is a great example of knowing what to do with the great hunger that burns in all of us. Just point it in the only direction where it can be fed: The Greatest Father of all. Thank you dad, I love you and I am grateful for your example, very grateful.

Mom, your passing sent quite a ripple in all of our lives. You loved fun and would go out of your way to find things that were funny and your laugh was contagious. The pursuit of fun in your life was an example that made this book possible. I'm sure you are now on the other side hearing me say "Thank you," as any well-mannered child would.

ACKNOWLEDGEMENTS

When she shows up at my house, well, my heart leaps. I did not know a baby could do so many wonderful things just by being alive. She brings joy to every minute I am around her, and I am only her grandparent. She teaches me so much about His love; I'm messed up over it. She has shown me how much my heart can expand and a pinch of insight as to how big His love must be and how patient He is with us. I sit for as long as she wants me, just holding her, talking to her and showing her whatever it is in the room that she wants to see. I am mesmerized by her, and I believe God's feelings aren't too different towards us except magnified at least a million times. I believe He loves it when we show up and are willing to be held by Him, talk to Him and bring our toys to show Him. I believe He loves it when we see ourselves within His vicinity. And He loves our smiles at Him, our free kisses and our penetrating stares of a child as we look to the One we trust. Yes, my granddaughter has taught me much about the Love of God for us and how delightful it is.

To my amazing support team that prayed me through this:

To my husband, even though you were working in Afghanistan during the writing of this book, your influence was felt in more ways than you will ever know. You are my husband and I love and appreciate you. Thank you for being so amazing.
Michelle G – you're the best. The right words in the right season and loving the book before it was born. Thank you!
Lisa, your continued encouragement and wanting to get your hands on it right away helped me through some doubting spots. You are a great sis!!
Ilona, the courage to tell me to soften up and love more and you were so right. Thank you!
Michelle M for encouraging me every chance you got and reminding me you were praying for me. That meant so very much to my heart.
Heather T, thank you for the help with the cover and the encouragement that you gave so freely.

Jessica, Kay and Sara Anne, Rachel, Nathanael, Carl, Brian, Ignacio, Aaron, who kept me going through their encouragement. The love and prayers were felt, thank you very much.

To my daughter, son and son-in-law who gave me the space to write and encouraged me when they could; thank you!

To my prayer group, Rebecca, Susan, Margie and Bill who spurred me on every morning we met. You are an invaluable part of my life. Thank you for being the family you have become.

To Doug, Brenton and Ken, you helped to get this started by the decision to set goals. Without you my dear brothers this book may have missed its timing. Thank you.

Felicity, thank you so much for the Foreword. You and Linda have always encouraged me to write, and that has meant a lot to me. Thank you to the both of you. I am grateful for our group of women and what we have done together.

Heather for wonderfully bugging me about when the book would be ready. I really did need that.

To the 60 day author group that kept answering my questions however trivial and who I had the privilege to support as well.

Felicia – what a great job editing, making me easier to read is no small feat. Thank you.

If you were not mentioned here know that you were not forgotten as I hold you in my heart as well.

CONTENTS

FOREWORD

God is fun!

Fun?

Really? We can have fun with God?

Christians aren't used to having fun--at least, not in a Christian context. I remember as a student, a friend of mine renting a gorilla outfit. He jumped over a wall, bananas clutched in hand, into a rather posh Christian party in someone's yard to see what would happen. Everyone ignored him. Not a smile. Nobody so much as raised an eyebrow. (Maybe they were used to gorillas turning up at their events!)

Juvenile, maybe! But it says something about us.

The God that many of us Christians serve is definitely serious, solemn, somber even. He's sitting in heaven wielding a big stick, waiting to catch us out in any slight misdemeanor. We obey Him out of a sense of duty. We live a life of "ought to's" and "shoulds."

We may not actually admit it to ourselves, but we Christians often behave as though God is a stern disciplinarian, to be feared and respected, rather than a loving, heavenly Father who delights to be with His children, who enjoys spending time in their company. He even sent the Holy Spirit to walk with us constantly. He created laughter.

Jesus is the image of the invisible God. If we want to know what God is like, let's look at Jesus. The ordinary people (not the religious ones) loved to be around Jesus. Children were happy in His presence. Notorious sinners chose to hang out with Him. People took time from their daily routines to spend time with Him, listening to His teaching, watching Him at work. They enjoyed being with Him.

Jesus didn't condemn people--think of the woman caught in adultery--but He taught them a different way to live. He lifted their burdens and lightened their loads. He promised them liberty and joy if they would follow Him.

It was the religious people who couldn't stand Jesus. His freedom was a huge contrast to their bondage to minutiae. Jesus loved to spend time in people's homes. Much of His teaching and many of His miracles occurred in the context of sharing a meal with them. In fact, His lifestyle was such that the Pharisees accused him of being a glutton and drunkard.

What was it about Jesus that was so winsome and attractive? I suspect, as Suzette Lambert so eloquently puts it in *Having Fun with God*, that Jesus was fun to be with. He was full of surprises, putting mud on the eyes of a blind person, sticking his fingers in the ears of a deaf mute. And they were healed! Life was never boring when He was around.

Most of us don't think of the Christian walk as "fun." Life is far more serious than that. Perhaps that's why the ideas expressed in *Having Fun with God* are initially shocking. God wants us to have fun? Part of the effectiveness of the book is in the use of the word "fun" rather than "joy." "Joy" is a word to which we have become so accustomed that we miss out on its deeper meaning. It's the shock value of the word "fun" when applied to our walk with God that brings us up short. It's not a word often used about God.

God, our Creator, created fun. He made humankind with a capacity for fun--for sheer enjoyment of life. It gives Him pleasure and delight when we have fun and experience joy with Him. The robbers of our ability to have fun with God are the tools that Satan uses--fear, anxiety, depression.

Suzette tackles these thieves of joy head on in this book.

I remember well the release I personally found when I learned to let God take care of various issues in my own life. He delivered me from fear. He dealt with various incidents that would replay again and again like a continuous-loop video in my memory. He set me free to enjoy His presence in new and fresh ways.

I've known Suzette for a decade or so. We worked together with others for several years on a book that examines gender equality in the church. I've watched her as she's walked through different trials along the way. I've seen her struggle in different areas of her life and finally come through to victory. Suzette is the real deal. So this is not merely a theoretical book. It's intensely practical, born out of her own personal experience as well as from her work as a licensed marriage and family therapist. This is also a vulnerable book as Suzette willingly shares her difficulties and how she's had to fight to overcome them.

Uniquely qualified to speak into these areas, Suzette presents a compelling case for a different kind of walk with God than many of us experience and she illustrates it with openness and grace.

Read and apply the principles of this book, and your walk with God might just include having fun with Him!

Felicity Dale
Author: *An Army of Ordinary People*;, Co-author, *Small is Big* and *The Black Swan Effect*
Austin, Texas.

INTRODUCTION

In graduate school they told us we would become relationship experts, which sums up the essence of being a marriage and family therapist. We study relationships and how they work, and we somehow find ways to improve them. Personally, my favorite relationship is with God. It's the relationship that makes the difference in every relationship we have.

Unfortunately I see too many people who struggle with their relationship with God. Now, a struggle is not a bad thing, in fact, it can be fun. We just tend to limit ourselves in our beliefs and never catch the thought we are actually having fun in the struggle. It tends to look more like "If I just do this right then this will be right." We might be putting more expectations on ourselves that will lead us to being disappointed and lost in our own expectations of ourselves. Well, I believe it is time to change all that.

That makes me a challenge to be around. People that spend any time around me eventually hear me say "that's cool" when they tell me their latest difficulties. When first timers hear me say it they look at me kind of funny and appear dumbfounded. Before they can catch their breath I usually say something about how great it is to be aware of the anxiety they are experiencing and how God can be with them in this fun time. People are often initially resistant, however many will venture with me into the fun zone.

You see, we create so much difficulty in our own mind. We describe things as difficult instead of finding a truly loving and trust worthy God that has already defeated the enemy. It's not that life is easy in the fun zone, but it might be.

I'm sure you will find yourself challenged here, as I was. Take up the challenge, as you are certainly worth it. Not because of what you do, but because of what Jesus did. That is good enough reason for you to be worth it.

As is any work the one who writes it must too be challenged by its words. I have been in this fun zone for a while, however even as I read it I realized how little I was in the fun realm compared to where I desire to be. I looked around the house realizing how many things I had neglected since starting the book. I then heard the words "whistle while you work" and I realized again, this is not about being alone, it's about having fun with Him even as I do the most mundane of tasks. Awe, what an amazing and awesome God we have.

The toughest part of this book was when I had finished it and while tying up the loose ends my mother died. I had to decide if I could have fun with God in the midst of going through all the emotional grief attached to losing a parent. What I am learning is that he is so very near, some days it's as if I feel His breath on may face as He holds me. His tenderness has never been so known by my heart, and that has changed everything, and I am even more convinced that God is fun.

Having Fun with God

PART I: THE BEGINNINGS

CHAPTER 1 YOU ARE MEANT TO SOAR

"One can never consent to creep when one feels an impulse to soar."

— Helen Keller, The Story of My Life

The first time we ever got in line for the ride, excitement flooded the air. Of course, at Disney, the line for a new ride has phenomenally long waits. This was no exception. We moved into the strange looking theater and were instructed to buckle up in seats that were different from the usual seats. I wondered what we were in for. It wasn't long before we were lost in simulated scenery, hang gliding over rivers, orange groves and pine trees. The scents to match poured into our air space, adding to the illusion. We left the room laughing and talking about how much each of us had enjoyed the ride as we shared highlights from what each experienced.

I have thought about that day multiple times since and, I am convinced we humans were meant to fly. Not just fly by mechanical means, but by means of fun, of release of the human spirit, not allowing ourselves to be tied down to our worries and concerns but to soar in who we are within this fun relationship with God.

Fun does not have to be a momentary condition that flitters away as if it was a butterfly caught on the wings of the wind. No. Fun, when grasped, has more substance than that. Fun has staying power. If you allow, it will bring you greater depths to your relationship with God. If you dare take the risk to dream of an amazing life filled with freedom and joy, then you will live your way into fun.

We, as humans, are attracted to fun. If this was not true, Disney would not be filling their parks with thousands of people every day willing to pay upwards of a hundred dollars in entrance fees. We are drawn to fun. People work fifty weeks a year to have two weeks of vacation so they can get away and smile for a while. College students get together (I know this because I presently live in a college focused town) and play video games, get drunk and laugh loudly because they want to experience fun. Children quit playing games if they are not having fun. We have a propensity towards fun, with the need for it tied up in our very health. In the last twenty years or more, the science community has been discussing the need for laughter and how it affects our health. We need fun.

My understanding of life is that I'm on a journey. And, this journey will continue long into eternity. My desire is to live wide open every minute of this life because of who lives in me.

"To them God willed to make known what are the riches of the glory of this mystery among the Gentiles: which is Christ in you, the hope of glory" (Colossians 1: 27, NKJV).

The part I really want you to focus on is the "Christ in YOU, the hope of Glory." To me, that is not a boring statement. If anything, it's inviting. It is filled with hope and excitement. When I read that verse, my internal dialogue is something like, "Christ in me. He's in me. Wow! The God of the Universe has given me the choice to allow Him to live in me. Oh, and it's bigger than that. Because while He has given me the choice to let Him live in me, my answer back is 'explode in me.' Hold nothing back because I know You are fun and You're going to break out new things in me and You are going to blow my mind and I am going to like it."

If you love amusement and fun, then you are at the right place. This is an adventure that will take you where you have not been before and you will find that God is brilliantly fun. I know not everyone is convinced that He is fun. I have learned most people would disagree with me. It's easier to choose following rules than to change the paradigm that gives way to the idea that He is fun. When we live with the rules and obey the rules, we have control. We fill ourselves up with pride on what we do. And, it is so easy to do. I know. Yes, I really know because I have been there. I still fight to leave that place of continual religious control. I still fight to find my way into a bigger, more open relationship that eliminates the darkness in my life which is usually my need for control. I like this place of relationship, where every day He looks at me with great delight and plans ways to bring me into closer relationship and greater merriment.

I have seen a shift, as of late, where the Body of Christ is appearing to grasp this. With greater awareness of who He really is, people are mentioning God is fun. This is a mind blowing realization happening amongst believers that has long been needed in the Body. Maybe it is even time for us to grab it and agree that yes, He is so much greater and multifaceted than we ever dreamed.

In my experience of this verse:

"But as it is written: "Eye has not seen, nor ear heard, Nor have entered into the heart of man The things which God has prepared for those who love Him"" (I Corinthians 2:9, NKJV).

I am drawn to begin to use my imagination. I open myself up to Him. "Come on, God. Blow my mind. Blow me away as to what You have planned for me. Show me what You will do. Bring it on."

And He responds:

"I know what I'm doing. I have it all planned out - plans to take care of you, not abandon you, plans to give you the future you hope for" (Jeremiah 29:11, The Message).

I want to engage with God and see what He wants to do. I like the idea of adventure that God has set before me. I have no idea how things are going to work. I simply trust that as I continue, He will show me how big and exciting He really is. I may not always like everything about it but I am learning to have fun in the midst of it all.

Chapter 2   Fun in the Relationship

I am a marriage and family therapist by trade. In my vocation, I have observed that people don't have fun anymore. It often takes at least two or three sessions before they are able to laugh, depending on the situation they have come in for. When people come for therapy, initially they don't laugh. They don't relate and often, they have gotten lost in the day to day struggle. This trend tends to be an overall outlook many have in their lives, not just the people I see. I am quite concerned about this and my desire is to see people increase their quality of life in Christ. I believe interaction with God in a more positive way will give us a greater desire to be involved with Him through out every part of our lives. When we do this, we will experience something different — perhaps something we may not have experienced since we were first saved.

We all had a honeymoon experience with God, or so I would presume. I hope you remember that feeling when you first found out God was what you had always desired. The euphoria of knowing your whole life had changed. Suddenly, God was a wondrous mystery you could not get enough of. As though you had been in the desert for years and stumbled across your first oasis, you wanted more. That passion was so fresh and delightful, so full of adventure. You were having fun with God. Sadly, within a few years, things changed. Life crept in and that choked out of faith feeling emerged. It's not that you didn't long for your first love anymore, it just seemed so impractical, unrealistic and out of reach.

It was to the church in Ephesus that Jesus sent this message:

"Nevertheless I have this against you, that you have left your first love. Remember therefore from where you have fallen; repent and do the first works, or else I will come to you quickly and remove your lampstand from its place--unless you repent" (Revelations 2:4-5).

Obviously, Jesus wanted the Ephesians to return to the place they started. I can't imagine them being any different in their beginning faith than the rest of us. Jesus knows what first love is—that amazing desire to be with someone, unable to apart from them, constantly desiring to look at their face, know their touch, and to always find being in their presence an adventure. First love is when the most exciting thing in the world is to spend time with the person of your heart and nothing can take its place. That is the door that is open to us right now, and on the other side is abundant pleasure.

So, what would happen if we all learned to have a different relationship with the One who created us? The One that is closer to us than our very breath. The One that desires to be with us, have conversation with us and laugh with us. What would happen if all of our relationship with Him was fun? What would happen if we enjoyed every minute of everything that has to do with Him? Wouldn't that be fun? And what would happen if we saw a church full of people who saw their relationship with God as fun? What if the entire body of Christ saw the adventure and fun in their relationship with Him? What would that look like? I believe the whole earth would explode with the glory of the Lord. Ah, do I dare to dream of such a day? I think so!!

Think about it. I'm sure it would be absolutely viral. This would change everything. It doesn't mean we would not mourn with those who mourn and comfort those who need comforting, but we would see all that as fun too. We would see God moving through us and doing what we have been waiting years for Him to do in us. We would comfort from our hearts in a way that would truly bring the comfort of Christ.

So, in the midst of all the pain and disappointments of life, it may be time to get going and start having a fun relationship with God. If that is your desire, it's time to take on a different way of thinking and decide that having fun with God changes everything. A different way of thinking is on the horizon. All you have to do is say yes to it and watch this new, vibrant, exciting relationship be birthed in your life. As you go further into this, you may decide there is no turning back.

Chapter 3 Is God Fun?

How would you answer the question, "Why is my relationship with God lacking fun?" What would you feel is at the heart of it all? Would you find yourself answering that God isn't fun? Or, perhaps you feel with all the work you have to do as a Christian to believe, how could you ever have any fun? Maybe you answered, "I've seldom seen Christianity as fun, and I don't see a lot of Christians having fun." Christianity is a way of life. It's rules we adhere to. It's a life we are chained to, a prison we are encased in. While those last two are a little extreme, you get my point.

It seems to me it is time for all those who are tired of a faith that binds them up in knots to release those ropes and drop them to the floor. It's time to address life differently and your faith is where you begin. It's like putting on a new set of glasses that allows you to see beyond where you see now. Or, maybe it's taking down the veil so you can see what you have never seen before. When Jesus died, the veil was torn in two. Can you imagine the people that were there and what it was like for them to be able to see into the Holy of Holies for the first time? I believe Jesus wants to tear off things that prohibit us from seeing with fascination the wonders of who He is. I also believe He wants to build us up so we can walk in sheer delight and inexpressible joy.

The initial premise involved in the idea of having fun with God is whether or not God is fun or whether God was stoic as He threw the stars into the sky and said, "Let there be light." Do you believe He grimaced as He watched Moses walk up the mountain? Do you think He elicited a cosmic whine of, "All right…if I have to," when the plan of salvation was devised?

This type of attitude from God seems quite unlikely. I cannot begin to fathom how big the smile on His face was when He said, "Let there be light." I believe it was easy for Him and that He chuckled all the time, often thinking of you and me. I think He even grinned as an angel or two stood watch with gaped mouths while He created something they had never seen before. Perhaps, that was part of the fun. Him observing the angels as He did all this. Actually, I think the angels are part of the fun of

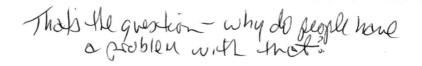

That's the question — why do people have a problem with that?

heaven. Imagine their responses all the time as they watch God. I wonder if they go *wow* continuously, like small children. Maybe God likes their reactions, even if He knows it will already happen. He is omniscient, after all.

I have heard multiple times that God must have a sense of humor. Just look at us. Still, I realize this might be quite a stretch for some people. So, what other proof do I have of God being fun?

Well, take Jesus for example. Jesus did say,

"If you had known Me, you would have known My Father also; and from now on you know Him and have seen Him" (John 14:7).

If we look through a lens where we presume God is not fun, one would have to ask, what was Jesus doing at a wedding? And what was He doing turning water into wine? Have you ever thought about that?

I once heard an internationally known speaker swear Jesus did not turn the water into wine. I thought that was presumptuous considering the Bible said He did. Besides, I'm not offended that He did, even if I choose not to drink. But, what is it about Jesus turning water into wine that initiates uncomfortable feelings on our part? What does it say to us about Jesus that we have not yet reconciled? If we struggle with this, perhaps it is time to take another look at what makes it a struggle.

And if we do not struggle with Jesus turning water into wine, what does this miracle say about Jesus? What is the conjecture we can make about Him that He even went to the wedding? What does it say about Jesus knowing He was okay with people getting a little tipsy on the wine? Jesus turned a lot of water into wine. With how uncomfortable the idea might make us, we would like to think He made that much wine for a 5000-person wedding. We could say maybe, but the closer truth is probably not. And how do we not know Jesus bringing the extra guests to the wedding (his disciples) wasn't the reason for the shortage in the first place? I would like to think that maybe Jesus's buddies liked enjoying themselves as well.

I have heard a gazillion explanations about that wine. Still, let's look at this. Have you ever gone to a Jewish event? I have. It was an exuberant bar mitzvah and the wine ran shamelessly. No one thought twice about how much they should have nor did they think about how much they should not have. They drank – not to get drunk – but as part of the merriment of the guests and the food and the festival. If a bar mitzvah is like that, how much fun must a wedding feast be?

In this, my thoughts are Jesus went to a wedding. He turned water into wine. He had a good time and those He went with had a good time too. He probably even cracked a smile as He initially walked towards the door of the place where the wedding feast was held. He might even have been thinking "Yup, this is going to be fun." I find it interesting that this is His first recorded miracle. It's as if God wanted to make sure we understood how important celebration was to Him.

This is just one place where we get a sense of Jesus having fun. There are other examples. I think this is pretty hard evidence.

Jesus hung out with tax collectors and sinners.

"The Son of Man has come eating and drinking, and you say, 'Look, a glutton and a wine bibber, a friend of tax collectors and sinners" (Luke 7:34).

That's what they said about him. A winebibber means one who drinks much wine. Jesus hung out with a crowd that people who were consumed by their own righteousness would never be around. Yet, that was the kind of people Jesus chose to be around. He wasn't manipulated into being with them, and He didn't follow the crowd as if He was without his own will. He purposely chose to be with them. He was also ridiculed for it by those who did not get it.

Another thought I had about Jesus being fun is the awareness that some of Jesus's closest friends were fishermen. I lived in a town for five years where fishing was one of the main industries. I learned a lot about fishermen during that time. I learned they have a lot in common with loggers, rednecks and millworkers. They tend to be a little rough around the edges. The ones on my block were adventurous and lived loudly and I would guess that fishermen like this are not a new phenomenon. My best bet is Peter, James and John were not so different.

Jesus was a carpenter. Maybe He had a shop in His house, or maybe He helped build houses like some of the carpenters we have now. Any way you look at it, He was a blue collar worker. He went looking for real men who were without pretentious ways. He went after men He could work with and train. Men who were not so lost in their own need to look perfect that they couldn't move on and enjoy life. These guys would be entertaining to break bread and eat fish with. They would not just work for him, they would be involved with Him and that was what He was looking for. Men who were fun to be with. These men would most likely laugh away the very things that would make others squirm because they were willing to look at life differently. They looked at life with a smile. They were not the social elite of the time. That wasn't what Jesus was looking for to begin this movement He was starting on earth. They were people who were connected and interdependent upon the relationships they had with one another and with Him. This would bring a different flavor to the whole earth.

I am pretty confident Jesus hung out with people that could laugh, smile and enjoy themselves. Why? Was it to bring them under the law? Hardly. People could have done that to them in their own culture. The Pharisees were quite capable of bringing nearly anyone under the law. I think Jesus wanted people who could laugh. People who could demonstrate who God really was and were relaxed and trustworthy enough to do that.

I also think God had fun in all His relationships in the Old Testament.

Enoch went somewhere. Now you see him, now you don't. Isn't that delightful?[i]

Joshua would not leave the mountain even though it was commanded that no one except Moses come up the mountain. Do you think God knew? Of course He did. I bet He smiled.[ii]

23

David was always imperfect, even before the Bathsheba and Uriah phase of his life. Still, God said he was a man after His heart. Wow, what a heart to love David so much.[iii]

God loved Solomon. God always knew Solomon would mess up, yet it did not stop God from loving him from the beginning. God is so merciful and so amazing.[iv]

It's not that God did not have His moments of anger with the Israelites, their kings and the tribes around them. Scripture says He did. However, God did not stay in His anger. He did what He thought was best and moved on. Part of the problem I see regarding this is so many people are convinced that God is still mad. They are not focused on the amazing redemptive act brought forth by Jesus. If all we have is an angry God, then where are we as people? Most likely we are running scared and afraid of what will come next.

Helping us move beyond the idea of an angry God, we see there is the wedding feast of the lamb that is recorded at the end of the book. And the wedding banquet that Jesus talked about where they went out into the highways and byways and brought people in. The one throwing the party wanted to make sure every chair was filled. Wow! For a God who is not fun, He is sure involved in a lot of partying. So what does that say? That says to me God loves to party. He loves lots of people at a party and He has every intention of making it a big bash.

Oh, and one more story. The one that has captured all of our hearts because we have all been him at one time or another. Be honest. Even if you have been saved all your life, you have had slippage. The prodigal came back home and his father threw him a feast. I have always been told this is a picture of God. Perhaps, we would all have been more comfortable with the story if the father would have rejected him. Or, at least presented him with a few conditions like, "Sure you can come back. But, you'll have to sleep in the barn and we'll see you first thing in the morning to get you started on your chores." No, that was not the father who greeted the prodigal. It was the welcoming father that kept a calf around for a lavish feast. Remember the brother heard a party going on and he was angry? He had restrained himself from partying. For what occasion? I believe the occasion was to show his father his piety. I wonder if his father would not have enjoyed the moment more if the oldest son had joined the party. Now, that would have been a delicious ending.

CHAPTER 4 CHOOSING THE ADVENTURE

My husband and I used to have business cards that read, "Adventurers." I loved watching people's reaction as they read the card. While we could have chosen to list our occupations or business, something in us had to put *adventurers*. It was, after all, the truth at that time. What we did not know was even putting it on the card was adventurous. The statement would become a bigger truth for us as we went on in our lives. It was in some of those adventurous moments that we truly found out how fun God was. Now, I am fully committed to the idea that God loves to have fun in the adventures.

My husband and I have had the privilege of going to many places all over the world. One such place is Bangkok, Thailand. Bangkok is an amazing city. I had never been any place quite like it before. It has lots of traffic. We arrived to Bangkok very tired from being on the train all day. We departed the train station in a taxi, knowing nothing about where we were going. We thought it would only take us a few minutes to reach the hotel we had booked for a couple of days. The idea of a comfortable bed buoyed us on. We sat there in the taxi as our driver headed in, what we trusted was, the right direction. Then we stopped. We stopped and we stopped. We stopped for so long, my husband and I wondered where the wreck was. We found ourselves becoming a bit impatient. The driver pulled out some snacks, offered them to us, showed us pictures of his family and kept a conversation going to divert our attention off of our own impatience the best he possibly could. When the cab began to move again, I figured we would go past an accident scene and see emergency vehicles everywhere. I was very surprised to discover all the waiting was caused by a light not in our favor. It was then we realized traffic lights in Bangkok were not set at the same length of time as the ones in our home of origin. When we stopped again, we were able to understand what the delay was about and could enjoy the trip.

I learned a very valuable lesson that day. Fun can be had in a taxi on the way to a hotel even when the light ahead is red. It's not about what is going on around you. It's about your attitude in the midst of everything.

Are you choosing to have fun or are you choosing to whine, complain and feel frustrated? Are you choosing to lighten up and enjoy the ride (or lack thereof) or are you going forward and choosing to be in the place of not being overwhelmed because things are not moving the way you think they should?

So is our walk of faith.

CHAPTER 5 MAKE THE CHANGE

I recently received news that my old car needs a lot of work. I've had it for nearly ten years and it is probably time for something to change. I don't want to go through all the work it takes to get a new car. I am often committed to keeping things the same, as I find many people are. We struggle with change. Although according to Heraclitus, it is the only thing that is constant. So, if the estimate for repairs comes in too high, I will have to decide what I am going to do.

We all live within this realm to some extent, often trying to decide if we can stay the same or if it is necessary to change and which will hurt the most. There's a few questions we often ask before we make any change. What if staying the same has too high of a price? What if staying the same comes with a bill on our health or a cost to our relationships? What if staying the same causes us to miss out on something dynamic and breathtaking? What if staying the same voids the opportunity to experience something we never thought was possible? Many of us think we don't have to change. We think other people need to change. Ha, I always laugh when I realize that. My thinking others need to change is the goofiest thing I can imagine. If a person is not enrolled in their own change, why should I hop on that bus and divert myself from my own need to change?

We may also wish our situation would change. I really dislike feeling stuck. It leads me to wishing something would change and help me out of feeling stuck, or bored and frustrated. When I do that, I realize I have made myself a victim. God invites me to change. Often, I expect Him to move first when, in fact, He already has. So, no matter how we feel about change, in order to experience a greater freedom in life, something has to change. Usually, it is us.

You may be asking, "What does this have to do with having fun with God?" Maybe it's when we get stuck that we don't see the fun side of God or our need to have fun. Maybe we belong to such a serious group that fun is rare and scarce in the rest of our lives as well. We do live in a very serious age, and we forget to have fun. To be honest, for some of us, it's easier to be serious than to have fun. There has also been this type of underlying theology (unspoken of course) that knowledge and seriousness is the next best thing to holiness, and may even be considered holy in certain circles. I'm not saying it isn't, and studying can be fun, as it is part of the adventure. *But, holding it all so intensely begins to make this faith feel more like a burden than a freedom.* It is said beautifully:

"Christ has set us free to live a free life. So take your stand! Never again let anyone put a harness of slavery on you" (Galatians 5:1, The Message).

"Keep company with me and you'll learn to live freely and lightly" (Matthew 11: 30, The Message).

Ah, it's like you can breathe when you see these verses. They are verses of promise and hope, not of carrying a heavy religion that feels exhausting. It's time to redefine what we are doing in this amazing relationship and be thrilled that we were saved. It's time to give up the penance of the past and receive this amazing delightful grace that can put a spring in our step and address our every thought on how we define our relationship with God.

CHAPTER 6 MAKING THE CHOICE

In my line of work I spend a lot of time with people who are considered to be mentally ill. Though, I'm not sure it is a fair label to put on anyone. When we label people, we tend to take away their sense of being able to make choices that change their life. Everyone has some awareness of being able to make a choice. We choose our clothes, our food, and our toothbrush. All of us, with rare exception, make many choices every day. Because we are creatures of habit that play within the rut of our usual lives, we often don't see them as such. Often times, we forget that we make choices. Instead, we label them as if we had no choice. "I had to wear this today because everything else was dirty. I had to eat this because there was nothing else in the house. I had to tell them that because I didn't want to hurt their feelings." So many choices we make. If I am honest about the clothes I wear, the choice I made was, "I chose not to wash clothes. I chose to do something else instead." Perhaps, because I held something else as more important, more pressing, but still I made a choice. Even as I sit here, I realize I can hear my clothes being cleaned by the washer. I got involved in something else and put them in the washer a little later than I had planned. They may be a little cold when I get to them in the morning and still a little wet, as I choose to hang all my work clothes up on the line. It may be a little uncomfortable for me in the morning. Still, it is a choice I made.

So, what does that have to do with having fun with God? Well, like most things, fun or seeing things as fun is a choice.

I remember being a part of a prayer deliverance team years ago. We helped people begin to find areas of growth and freedom in Christ. It was an odd night and the people we were working with were particularly wounded. I had a friend on the team look at me and say, "Now isn't this fun?" At the time, I thought she was a little crazy. I had not yet adapted the idea that God was fun and I was a little concerned about her stance towards this. I realized she was asking me to look at it differently. All I was seeing was the wounds of the people we were working with. She was seeing the potential. I eventually caught on, although looking at a mess was initially a stretch for me. I learned to look past the wounds and see the potential in people and in their future. I learned to see the hope we both were looking for. I chose to spend less time seeing people for their painful, broken places. I saw them for what they were in that moment, for what was about to happen in their lives and how amazing that would be. Everything can change in a short amount of time. All I had to do was say yes.

It's interesting to me that God chose to give the gift of salvation for free. All it takes is a choice. The choice is to accept Jesus forever. The freedom involved in this free gift is absolutely superb. To think that God is giving a free gift to have a relationship with each individual on the earth is staggering to me and to think He spends time and resources to make sure I say yes to it blows me away. How could I say no to such an offer? Obviously I could not because I am lost in His magnificence. The goodness of this God fascinates me. Being in relationship with Him is so fun to me. I am blown away by this offer.

Some time ago, at a restaurant for a friend's birthday, I was asked what I thought of the conversation, actually an ongoing discussion for a couple of years, between two people. One said we do not have a choice in how we feel. My friend said we do have a choice in how we feel. He asked me my opinion. I said "Yes, we do have a choice on how we see things." The one responded, "I think that is (expletive)." My reply, "That is your choice." My friend laughed at my response. But to be honest, I think choices are one of those sparkles in life. I remember during the Cold War hearing about how people lived in the former Soviet Union. I once saw newsreel clips of people standing in line to get groceries at a store. They had no choice on what kind of bread they ate. There was only one type. They had no variety on any of the products they received. Even though they had to wait in long lines, there was no guarantee the store would have what they needed by the time they got inside. Their reality was they had no choice. If they did get in the door, it was either get what was offered or do without. Coming from this perspective, we see that having a choice can be fun.

Belief in choice is detrimental to all of us. People who don't believe in choice tend to see themselves as victims, living life without dessert, receiving the basics. I believe an attitude of entitlement comes out of a sense of having a lack of choice. How does that work? When you think you are without choice and unable to take care of yourself, the only option is to insist others take care of you. The myth has deceived the mind to believe their world is against them and that nothing will or can work out, so someone must do something for them or they are sunk. It comes with a sense of urgency and fear, which is not conducive to a productive and full life.

We all have places where we believe we are without a choice. It's only when we decide to flip our own thinking patterns that we can win and play a different game in life. As a result, our relationships will change, our lives will change, our attitude will change and most importantly our relationship with God will change. We do live with a much greater God than we ever imagined. There is no waiting in line. There is no one size fits all relationship that we can have with him. He gives us choices and He loves us in the midst of it all. To me that is fun.

Chapter 7 Fear and Fun

Some may have problems reconciling the idea that we are to fear God with having fun. It's an interesting thought to adore God and fear Him. We can have fun with Him and have reverence towards Him all in the same moment. One does not negate the other. What if we began to look at that differently? What if we actually began to look at learning the fear of the Lord as fun? The fear of the Lord is not the same as being afraid of Him. It's embracing the all surpassing majesty of His greatness and having the utmost respect for it. What if we went into this great love He has for us and had delight in it? What if we decided that the process of learning greater fear of the Lord was fun? What if we looked into His eyes and said, "I fear you and that is so exciting?" I love playing the game Your way, God. Your game is so much funner (I know it's not a word, but it should be) than mine. How can I not fear you? How can I not respect you? How can I not adore you for all that you are? How can I not find this fun as I am in the process of being made into the likeness of your Son?

Oops, now I have gone and spoiled it. It's difficult to think about how He creates in us the image of His Son, because if we have paid attention in the past that was never fun. Or was it? Let's take a glimpse:

"Looking unto Jesus, the author and finisher of our faith, who for the joy that was set before Him endured the cross, despising the shame, and has sat down at the right hand of the throne of God" (Hebrews 12:2, NKJV).

What did the author say? For the joy that was set before Him. We are the joy that was set before Him. We were in the steps He took that were, at times, difficult. I am not saying Jesus skipped to the cross. There are also times we realize skipping seems impossible. Times when we are more likely to crawl. Keep in mind, a crawl can seem important and can appear fun when it is all over with because of what was gained in the process.

I went through a period of multiple miscarriages. I could not carry a baby beyond two months. I felt hopeless and hurt. More than anything, I wanted to have more children. I had one child at the time, but the view I had of my life included more. I walked through this season with a deep sense of isolation as I grieved deeply. I felt no one understood me. While I became angry at God, I was also more dependent on him than I had ever been. As I sat rocking and singing Jesus loves me, He was my source of comfort. I also felt He was the source of my pain as He had allowed the children, I so desperately wanted, to die.

One day in my anger, I cried out, "What do you want from me?"

His answer surprised me. "Get ready, you are going back to school."

Now I had a mission, which is important to me. I feared Him enough to know what He said was the best plan for my life. The doctor told me there was nothing more he could do for me with regards to the miscarriages and we did not have the finances to take the process any further, so I shifted my focus.

I began to look at colleges. We moved to another state where I continued my education. My husband also switched careers. I graduated with my Bachelor's degree six months pregnant. Going to school addressed a lot of the thoughts and feelings I had about myself and God that were very overwhelming for me at that time. God used the miscarriages to write my future differently and I am forever grateful. I am not sad for the children I lost as they will never know this world of sin and I am sure they are perfectly happy.

Now, I have a different perspective on that time. When I was in the middle of it, I felt hopeless and isolated due to much of my own thinking. I can look back now and see that period as a time of great importance where God in His wonderful goodness and great kindness used my disappointment to give me direction that changed our lives. I believe this:

"To console those who mourn in Zion, To give them beauty for ashes, The oil of joy for mourning, The garment of praise for the spirit of heaviness; That they may be called trees of righteousness, The planting of the Lord, that He may be glorified" (Isaiah 61:3, NKJV).

I believe He comforts and supports all of us. He gives beauty for ashes. At least that is what He has always done in my life. I have also seen Him do this in the lives of others. When we look back and see that He has sustained us through difficult times, given us provision in the midst of pain, or been there in the worst of it, we can say, "Yes, what He did was fun. Even though, it did not always feel fun in the moment."

Chapter 8 Taking a Different Look

Some people might ask if having fun with God is compromising. Some may even think it takes the seriousness of our faith out of the equation. We only compromise when we give in to a place that exonerates darkness. In having fun with God, not only do we not absolve darkness, we actually give way to light. Paul says it well:

"You've all been to the stadium and seen the athletes race. Everyone runs; one wins. Run to win. All good athletes train hard. They do it for a gold medal that tarnishes and fades. You're after one that's gold eternally. I don't know about you, but I'm running hard for the finish line. I'm giving it everything I've got. No sloppy living for me! I'm staying alert and in top condition. I'm not going to get caught napping, telling everyone else all about it and then missing out myself" (I Corinthians 9: 24-27, The Message).

So, learning to have fun is a discipline of its own type. It's also a choice. It's a choice to remove the somber, unexciting way people experience their faith. It's about becoming contagious, not by denying the truth but by looking at the truth through a brilliant light.

As a therapist, I have learned to look at every circumstance through many different eyes. *What I have learned is that perspective is everything.* Attitude matters. This is what I am encouraging here. The ability to go from feeling like a victim, or one who is hopelessly tied to a God who would burden us with works, to experiencing amazing success and relief. To be able to look at the relationship with adventure in a way that produces fruit even as it delights each party involved.

Here is the challenge of this book. Look at your relationship with God differently. Look at it with infinite possibilities instead of something boring, or worse yet as being locked in a jail waiting judgement. Look at it as an opportunity to be loved in a new way instead of believing you are only conditionally or marginally loved. Get a new revelation of who He is instead of believing what you have always believed and been disappointed by as a result. See what He is working in you and consider that you have never experienced this new place in Him before.

PART II THE FOUNDATION

CHAPTER 9 BUILDING THE FOUNDATION

In this chapter, I am going to begin to build on what is foundational for turning your relationship into fun. Please remember this is a process and perfection is never required. These components will help give fun a backbone so you can take your relationship with God to a whole new level. If you find you are missing any of these or you feel you need more of them, my challenge to you is just ask God. I know. That is pretty simple. But, I also know I often avoid asking.

One night, I was going somewhere and I was thinking about things I wanted. I heard Holy Spirit say very clearly, "You want much, but you ask little." The verse that immediately came to me was:

"Yet you do not have because you do not ask" (James 4:2b).

That was a very startling moment for me. I realized I might want many things. However, if I never ask, I don't know what I am keeping myself from. It is important to feel free to ask for what you want. Ask for what you believe you need in order to change your relationship with God into an amazing adventure where you find excitement around every corner.

When we think of getting something, we often go into the how do I make that happen. It's really how we as a society think. We believe that if I do A, then B will result. An example would be: A) I go to work and then B) I get a paycheck. This will work a little differently. More along the lines of, if I begin to address and absorb A into my life, then all these other things will happen. In a nutshell, it's Matthew 6:33:

"But seek first the kingdom of God and His righteousness, and all these things shall be added to you."

It's not an A then B equation, it's more of pursue this life and then this life that you want will happen. All the foundation blocks to building a life of fun are Kingdom of God properties. They are a result of Kingdom thinking and will result from a Kingdom lifestyle, which is about seeking the King and His plans. When you do, so much more than you ever thought was possible will happen.

There are components that assist in creating greater atmosphere for fun in our lives. Once we have accepted these into ourselves, as if we were accepting the Holy Spirit (which we are), we find we allow access to move us into a different space that will make us wide open to living within a world of fun. These are not mechanical how tos. *They are ways of being*, of becoming, which is the most effective way to address fun. Fun is something that is birthed out of a deeper place than how do I do this. It's birthed from a depth where we can smile and enjoy ourselves without making it happen. It's often spontaneous, more of a tribute to who we are within our relationship with Him than what we did to make something happen.

I believe there are something like foundation stones that present an open door for fun. Each of them is powerful, and together they are unbeatable. When we accept them into our lives we find that we bring God everywhere and have fun while we are doing it. I love the number five because to me it has always meant grace. Grace is truly one of my most loved words as it is powerful and able to change any situation in an instant. So, the grace that is necessary for you to walk in these foundation stones (building blocks) is being loosed for you to grab them and run with them.

I'm not saying you have to accept all these building blocks to have fun. They are included because they strengthen the potential for over the top exuberance. Who doesn't want that? The choice of each is for good reason, which I am sure you will agree. They are foundational to our Kingdom lives. They each present possibilities, which open doors to more awe and wonder. When you are done reading this, most likely you will come up with a couple of your own. It would be a great idea for you to grab whatever you can because He wants to give it to you.

You may notice the first three fruit of the spirit are mentioned as building blocks. These manifestations of fruit are the result of walking with Holy

Spirit. Just as you would hopefully have fruit in any investment, a life spent with Holy Spirit will produce fruit. If you want to know how to increase in this, spend time with Holy Spirit. That is how you do it. When you do, you will be in the best of company. I have learned over the years that spending time with Holy Spirit isn't just quiet time, although it is that. It can be so much more.

"Trust in the Lord with all your heart, and lean not on your own understanding; in all your ways acknowledge Him, and He shall direct your paths" (Proverbs 3:5-6).

This is the day to day, moment by moment walk that changes everything. It's the awareness of Him always being there and so the internal conversation is continual although not always chatty. I guess for me, it's the recurring exchange that has a life of its own which invites me closer to him, desiring his thoughts and my openness to whatever He has for me. This is what produces the fruit of the Spirit in my life.

I used to think the fruit of the Spirit was something I had to create in myself. As I continue in this walk, I look back and see how flesh filled my walk with God has been. I'm sure you understand what I mean. I was willing to change, but it had to look like what I thought it should look like. I worked at creating the fruit of the Spirit I thought I wanted so badly. This fruit was rotten. Take love, for instance. It was conditional. Joy was about working to make myself happy, by controlling my external settings instead of receiving a presence of the work of the Holy Spirit. Peace was only attainable when everyone else cooperated. Because all of this was more about misery than living in a place of rest, I was often anxious and worrisome and worked on changing other people all the time.

Eventually, I learned this was not Kingdom living and for me this kind of life was not helpful. God showed me that I could trust Him and watch the fruit appear in my life. I never had to ask for patience, Holy Spirit took my hand as I worked with people who were difficult for me to understand. I did desire some fruit more than others, even as you may enjoy an apple more than an orange (or vice versa). This has been helpful as I wanted to learn love from God's perspective. I am still learning, and I still love the process. Loving difficult people is a great growth exercise. My love muscles have grown and the weight of it has gotten so much lighter. Mostly because I have learned I don't have to lift the weight of loving people alone. Holy Spirit is my spotting partner and not only do they and I not fall, if I open my eyes during these sessions, I see that He is actually holding their weight for me.

CHAPTER 10 BUILDING BLOCK #1 LOVE

So if I speak in tongues of men or of angels but have not love, I'm noisy and don't bring with me what I was called to bring. Okay, honesty sometimes stinks. Love is important.

I have observed in working with people that no one can love well until they can receive love. My story is not different. You see, I too had to learn to receive love. For a long time in my life, I believed love was conditional. I also believed God needed me to perform for Him. If I successfully carried out whatever task I perceived He had for me just right or just enough, then He would love me more or He would bestow some wonderful gift on me. I was so very ignorant about His love and to be honest, I was a mess internally. In His great patience, He helped me realize not only did He love me, but He decided I was loveable. You see, I knew I was loved. I just left it out there at arm's length and never allowed it to come into me. When I realized I was loveable, not because of what I had done, but because of what He chose to do, then I could become a sponge, able to receive this amazing love. I believe I am not the only one with this story.

This realization changed my life. The idea of being loveable changed everything, because I could finally place value on me. Many people do not find value in themselves. In my field, they call it low self-esteem. From my experience, low self-esteem is tiring. It's exhausting when someone thinks so little of themselves. Low self-esteem is the result of not being able to receive love. *When you are able to accept love, you begin to find value in yourself. Or maybe, once you find value in yourself you can accept love.* I'm not sure exactly how it will work for you. It may be both in the same moment. It was for me.

I also find it interesting that people do not find value in themselves. The enemy (the devil, satan) puts enough value on us to dedicate his limited resources to make our lives miserable. The enemy will do just about anything to tear us away from the love the Father has for us. He will steal, kill and destroy to make that happen. He will tell us we are not loveable and not valuable. He will continually inform us that we are not worthy of

God's love. He does this all while working to undermine our faith and ability to receive love. I do not completely understand his payoff, other than He hates us because the Father loves us. In the midst of this, I prefer to look at how valuable I am to Father. There is a fun piece to this in Romans 8 at the end of the chapter. Paul asks what can separate us from the love of God. He concludes, nothing. I have pretty much declared in my life since nothing can separate me from the love of God, I might as well accept it. To accept love is to say yes to a life of love and quests unknown. It's to embrace yourself and your Creator in one fell swoop that breathes life into your very being. It's to say yes to all that is wonderful. To find yourself in another dimension that opens doors leading to greater delight. To say yes to love is to say yes to your future.

When I look at His decision to declare I am valuable, valuable to the point that He sent Jesus to rescue me from my own self, I fall madly in love with Him all over again. Within this realization, I make the decision to trust His plan and purpose for my life. In making this choice, I am presented with a hope and a future.

I have a loved one I talk to about the love of God frequently. When I speak of this love poured out for them they often say, "I don't know about that." This seems so sad to me as they appear to be unable to grasp what God has for them. They can't grasp the amazing love He wants to pour over them so they can know His love and be released from so much of the pain they experience by not accepting the love of God. You see, we love with such a shallow love when we do not accept love. Or, we accept love conditionally. Love that is unconditional brings acceptance to the person that is being loved and the person who loves. Conditional love brings a sense of judgement and rejection with it. People who are conditional in love usually start with being conditional towards themselves.

We are all conditional in our ability to love. Only God is unconditional in His love towards us. Someone I knew said when they were deep in sin they still felt loved by God. And, they were right as nothing can separate us from that love. It is unfortunate that so few know it. We are more likely to make God's love for us conditional because we are conditional in our ability to love. It's only when we set our minds on His love for us and embrace it that we begin to change. We then learn the fun of loving without condition in a way that we never have before. It's a way that brings peace.

Love changes everything. Without love, life has no ability to be fun. We were made for love. We were made to receive and give love. When we receive love, everything changes. When we learn to love well, again, everything changes.

Loving well is an art. It's living from I Corinthians 13 with the decision of living in it every moment. It's the resolve to give up offense and not put a condition on the love we receive as well as give. Not all of us know when someone loves us. Deciding to accept that you are being loved will alter every circumstance in your life. The place to start is to say to God, "I accept You love me and I accept Your love for me and I ask that You will create in me the ability to love." Continue to listen as you pray this prayer, it will happen. This is process, you and God's process and it's exciting. He will lead in this dance if you allow him.

CHAPTER 11 BUILDING BLOCK #2 JOY

I love joy. It's to life what garlic is to Italian cooking. Some people think garlic is a spice. I believe the Italians got it right. Garlic is an ingredient. Joy is something buried so deep in us that when we grab it, we become more emotionally even. When we are losing our balance, it gives us something to hang on to. It's the essence of the living waters that are to flow out of our bellies. Joy makes everything taste better in life.

Joy isn't superficial smiling. It's not just momentary laughter. It is present as if it has a mind of its own. Joy is an ongoing lightness that permeates our beings. It grows with time and becomes more pervasive as we walk with God. It's not happiness, although that can be an outcome. It's joy and to describe it singularly is impossible.

Before joy became my friend and stuck around, I had only caught glimpses of it. It felt like it always went somewhere else and kept someone else company. I would look at people and envy them because they had something more resilient in their being than I did. It was something that made them surer of themselves and more trusting of themselves and other people. I didn't know it was joy. I had no idea. Joy is one of those essentials of life that make this Christ filled life so breathtaking.

I was one of those people that had to be hit with joy, and I mean hit. I was in a church one day and God in his great kindness had someone pray for me. I had a supernatural experience where I got hit so hard with joy I laughed for forty-five minutes as a wall held me up. It was a curious thing to stand there and belly laugh for that long. However, when the laughter subsided, I experienced this amazing relief from worry and fear. I began to look at the promises of God with greater certainty. I looked upon Him with greater confidence in His ability. That was probably the best laugh I had ever had.

If the joy I experienced in that moment had left, I would have been disappointed. It has stayed to varying degrees these last fifteen years. The degrees only vary depending on my emotional state, not God's. If I choose to stay in a trusting state, I am more likely to experience a greater depth of enveloping joy.

Joy doesn't just affect our lives. It also affects the lives of others and tends to add to the fun of life. In the 1970's, I remember singing a song that was such a great truth, but I was more caught up in the hand movements than I ever was in the revelation of the words. Maybe some of you are familiar with this rendition of it:

"Joy is the flag flown from the castle of my heart,
From the castle of my heart, from the castle of my heart
Joy is the flag flown from the castle of my heart
When the King is in residence there
So lift it high in the sky let the whole world know,
Let the whole world know, let the whole world know
So lift it high in the sky let the whole world know,
That the King is in residence there. "

I love that this song says joy is a flag. People with joy going on in their lives are delightful to be around. They take a heavy moment and make it lighter. People's mood can change when someone that walks in joy enters the room. It is a flag that people without it are drawn to. Joy is something that is written within us as a result of Holy Spirit showing us great Kingdom truths.

Are you willing to find out how abundant joy can be? Would you like to discover how God does not withhold any good thing from His children? Joy is a good thing, a wonderful thing. It makes us conquerors. It makes us lovers of God with gusto. It produces passion in our lives. This ingredient changes everything. We become more because we see more as possible. Jesus went to the cross for the joy that was set before him. Joy is a sustainer in the worst of times.

What do you do if you feel like you don't have enough joy? I think asking for more is the appropriate response. Just be ready for it to show up!

What do you think is the difference between joy and fun? I find joy to be a constant in this life. It's just there. It holds us and keeps us. It is part of this walk. It's filled with hope. Without it, we often find ourselves dry and bored, submitted to a lackluster life.

Fun on the other hand can be the extra sparkle found in every given situation. It's the knowledge that not only will everything work out but there will be delight along the way. Fun is the unexpected that brings that extra smile. It's the ability to say to ourselves, "Oh, this walk is so surprising in the midst of what is going on and I don't have to make anything happen."

CHAPTER 12 BUILDING BLOCK #3 PEACE

This is ballast for me. It's my stabilizer. Peace keeps me in a place of surety in the midst of tumultuous moments. It's a plan that helps me move beyond my present circumstances. It's forward moving in the storm and the presence of stillness within the quagmire. Peace disrupts my mind in quiet ways when activity around me requires I become what I cannot be. *Peace is the promise of the moment passing when I am in great difficulty.* Peace grounds me so I can hear where I am not. Peace presents itself in great kindness. Peace is a craving when all around me is chaos.

Peace adds to fun. You see if there is no peace, then anxiety is what is producing the moment. You'll look for fun and all you will really get is more anxiety. When you feel anxious, there is no such thing as sustaining fun. It will be illusive under these circumstances and perceived as a way of getting out of the pain of the anxiety. Fun is not about running from something that makes us uncomfortable for a momentary fix. Fun is longer lasting than that and peace helps to strengthen it and make fun possible. Isaiah 26:3 says:

"You will keep Him in perfect peace, Whose mind is stayed on You, Because He trusts in You."

What an amazing thought, the possibility of peace all the time. Don't you love that idea? It's when He is our focus that we are able to find that ballast, that balance that keeps us from sinking in the midst of a storm. It keeps us choosing what is best and looking at things through His eyes. Peace is impressive, and it's attached to talking and walking with Him.

"For He Himself is our peace, who has made both one, and has broken down the middle wall of separation" (Ephesians 2:14).

He's the one that holds us there when we are open to Him, His ways and His thoughts. We may have to ask to learn the road of peace. It's a road filled with fun challenges. If you look at it as a game, a challenge you were meant to win, then you will. If you look at it as though God creates these challenges to leave you in the dust, then you may experience that as well. That would imply there's an opportunity for your paradigm of God to be updated to a God who deeply loves you and is committed to your success.

I would suggest you don't give up. Fight for your peace by pursuing the Lord for it. It's not really a fight, because you know He wants you to succeed. Put on those shoes of peace and find out how strong you are in the Lord. You are an amazing warrior. You can do this and you will be delighted in the undertaking.

Peace will be with you so you can have fun in the storms.

It was a big storm — an amazing storm, one of the greatest tests of my life. We had one of those business failures as a result of the housing market changing in Florida where we lived at the time. We were about to lose everything. We were trying to figure out how to eat. I found the quickest job available. Amazingly, in the midst of it all, I was fairly peaceful. It all eventually led to me living in Georgia and my husband working in Afghanistan. All things we never expected, yet we knew He was in them. Even in the midst of this huge, potentially devastating storm, He guarded us with His peace.

CHAPTER 13 BUILDING BLOCK #4 THE CHOICE OF FREEDOM AND FREEDOM IN THE CHOICE

During my time as a counselor, one of the most difficult and daunting tasks I have had is to work with people who feel they are choice less. The thing I have noticed about people that feel they have no choice is that they believe they are victims. This is a very difficult place for anyone to be. It also gives way to a miserable attitude and a bitter heart.

I have learned the more I believe I have a choice, the more likely I am to make the best choices as I talk to God about these choices. Even as we talk about the choices, He lets me know I have a choice. He may nudge me. But, I get to say yes or no to his nudge. Either way, I have a choice.

I also have a choice about a lot of things I may not think I have a choice on. I have a choice about what to think and how to feel about a situation. Don't believe me? That is your choice. And these choices all come with the amazing choice to ask the question, "Am I going to find this all fun?" Will I begrudgingly do what He is taking me down the road to do or will I gladly do it and find fun along the way?

The funnest (I know (sigh), it is not a word) thing of all is the ability to find it fun. Fun is not a constant unless you begin to switch your paradigm to see that what you are in the midst of is fun. Not because you don't see the reality of the situation, but because you choose to see the potential in the situation. Are you willing to see what you see? Or are you willing to put on heaven's perspective and see the fun in any given moment as the Kingdom moves in the earth?

"Is heaven's perspective fun?" I would gather that if God is fun, then all of heaven must follow suit. He is not incongruent! I believe there is so much going on and coming out of heaven that they are having fun all the time. Angels rejoice in heaven when a person gets saved. That sounds like fun to me. It appears to me God is always having fun and yet He is so comfortable in the gravity of difficult situations, not making light of them. I know He draws near to the broken hearted and in that He finds great satisfaction. What if there is more to Him than we think? What if He actually enjoys all that He does? That would make Him different than anyone I know. I want to live like that too!

As a culture, we are caught up in the pressure of everyday life. In recent years, we have become a weekend oriented society. I think the phrase, "I can't wait for the weekend," has been heard and said by most people. We discuss the day of the week all the time. "Oh, it's Monday," we say with dread. Then, it's Tuesday, which at least is not Monday. Then, we have hump day and almost Friday (Thursday). Finally, we arrive to, "Thank God it's Friday." People live their lives and adjust their moods dependent upon the day of the week. We whine, moan, complain and shout for joy depending on the day. We are lost in that weekend drift of life.

I wonder if God looks forward to weekends. I wonder if He can hardly wait until Fridays. Ponder if He has fun in all of His moments and does not wait until the weekend to finally enjoy Himself. I would speculate that He enjoys his work and does not conceive it as work as we know work to be. Most likely, it is an out flow of all that He is and once again He is always creating fun. Imagine God saying, "Yup, it's time to take a holiday. I think the weather might be great this time of year in another galaxy." I don't really see that happening. He holds the whole world in His hands. The fantastic thing is He does it all as an outpouring of His love which is endless. He would never have to speculate on his own needing rest. He is perfect rest.

In the place I work, I wanted to quit for a long time. Holy Spirit eventually talked to me about how it was the most productive time of my week, which I did not really want to believe. It's during my work that I am able to touch the most lives and reach out to the most people. It's also the time when the anointing in my life can be the strongest because He has given me what I need to be there. Now, I go into work every day choosing to take His word for it, and I believe He is right.

CHAPTER 14 BUILDING BLOCK #5 THE THANKFUL LIFE

I learned about being thankful when I was down. God used my work environment to bring me to this place. As a result, I am forever grateful to Him for opening my eyes.

At the time, I hated the job I was in. I wasn't the only one. Everyone there pretty much hated it. I did not care for my boss either. Even though I could explain their behavior and justify my feelings, I felt choice less and trapped. I woke up every morning feeling despair. One morning, I woke up and felt once again like I hated my life, a result of hating my work. I felt the dread of having to get ready for a job I did not like. I heard Holy Spirit say very clearly, "What are you going to do?" I knew in that moment He was asking me what choice I was going to make.

My brain wanted to continue down the same path of hating my job and justifying it all based on other's behavior. However, I realized I could follow that or I could decide to change something. Not in them, in me. This was my decision point. Decision point is a place where you make a choice and everything changes. My revelation was to change my mood through thanksgiving.

It was one of those moments when worlds seem to collide and the most powerful remained intact. My faith, by the power of the Holy Spirit, erupted in every movement I made. I nearly hopped out of bed. I began to recite all the things I was thankful for, even some I was not but was willing to make the venture towards. I thanked Father for my job, for my boss, for each person there and for other things in my life. Initially, I was excited. However, in this process, the sudden feeling of being stilted came over me. I felt like I could not go any farther. I felt the wall come upon me. I knew I either had to push through or I was going to go to work hating the place again. Again, I was at a decision point. I began to be thankful for all the little things I could think of. I continued through my morning being thankful.

I had heard sometime before, if you begin your thanksgiving in the first ten minutes of your morning, you will change your day. Well, I changed my life. I found myself choosing to change my attitude about my work.

Sometimes with the things I saw, I wondered if everyone else thought I was delusional. I kept insisting I was going to be thankful.

Thankfulness became a way of life for me after that. My prayer group probably got tired of me going on and on about all the things I was thankful for. I grabbed onto Psalms 100:4:

"Enter into His gates with thanksgiving, And into His courts with praise. Be thankful to Him, and bless His name."

And I would not let go of it.

I later went to a conference that revealed the power of thanksgiving. It was mentioned that people who are thankful are less likely to be depressed. If people are depressed, thanksgiving can be used as a tool to get them out of depression. I know this for a fact, because I see people's lives change as they press into a place of thanksgiving. Thanksgiving is not just for November anymore!

"In everything give thanks; for this is the will of God in Christ Jesus for you" (I Thessalonians 5:18, NKJV).

It does not say for everything, although somedays that may be necessary. Being thankful in everything gives God an opportunity to flip it. When I thanked God for a boss I did not like, I saw Him flip it. Eventually, He gave me a boss I did like and also created a more satisfying relationship with the boss that at one time I did not like. God is a redeemer. But, sometimes we are the one that opens the door –with His help and permission – to watch everything change.

Remember this is not a religious exercise. This is actually elating. When I pushed past my feeling that I did not want to do this, I released something in the spirit realm. It felt like I could fly. Giving thanks for my boss and all the other people gave me room to forgive them and push past my need to wallow in my own self-pity.

Things definitely changed. My brain began to accept thanksgiving as a way of life. Oh, and in time, the feeling in the office changed too.

"Be anxious for nothing, but in everything by prayer and supplication, with *thanksgiving,* let your requests be made known to God; and the peace of God, which surpasses all understanding, will guard your hearts and minds through Christ Jesus." (Philippians 4:6-7, NKJV).

Even as I placed living a thankful life as part of the fun combo, Paul has placed it as elemental to the amazing peace he mentions in this verse. Thanksgiving, is important. It is not to be trifled with. When you allow it to explode through your life, people will notice and you will bring this energy into their life. Thanksgiving is contagious. Just try talking to people about how grateful you are and see what happens.

PART 3 LET'S BEGIN

Chapter 15 Moving Past the Religious Life

I have been religious all my life. Within the scope of this book, I define religion as a way of making myself acceptable to God by following rules and choosing, at times, what would appear to be superstitious habits. Doing these religious behaviors negates the relationship have with Father, as if what I do which is right in my eyes will create the intimacy I am looking for. I am confident I am not the only one that does these types of things. The Pharisees and Sadducees of Jesus's day were pros at following the rules and locking people into a religious lifestyle. In our day, we live like we're trying to make up for something. As if the separation from God that took place in the Garden of Eden has made it so much easier to be self-dependent than God dependent – or so we think. We have tilled the soil. We have methods for everything. We live on methods. In my religious way of doing things, I am convinced if I do enough prayer, if I do enough righteous acts or if I do enough giving, God will surely be on my side. Some of that is valid, as we reap we sow[v]. However, to be superstitious about our walk and not have it birthed out of our relationship with Him makes it a heavy burden.

We can get so caught up in our methods and doing Christian life right that we forget to have fun. I find many Christians are so busy with going to church or the next conference, or taking care of the latest mission or…. (the list goes on) that they seldom take time to enjoy, relax and embrace something other than the urgent. We get so caught up in the method, we forget to smile or greet someone from the heart. Notice I said from the heart! We all have our 'we're out in public' face. When was the last time you chose to enjoy a laugh or pay attention to the beauty of nature? When was the last time you stopped and smelled a flower or just enjoyed the moment of standing in the sun? When did you eat outside last and made it a moment of pleasure? When you did this, did you talk to God? Did you talk to Him about how wondrous He is and how you enjoyed His presence at that moment? Maybe you didn't talk to him. Maybe you just knew He was present. In that moment, you were connected and it was more than enough.

Religion, with all its *I have to do this and I have to do that,* keeps us out of rest and pleasure. It prevents us from perceiving what fun could be. Religion is a hope stealer. It tends to keep us bound up and unhappy, all the while doing our best to please a god we perceive as not having fun either. I think people believe God does not have fun, so in some way we are forbidden as well. That makes life kind of difficult. Trying to use religion to monitor our relationship with God gets us stuck in what is right as opposed to being with Christ, which is very different.

Yes, being with Christ! That is totally different from what is right – or what we perceive to be right. I think we often get lost in what we think is good. One time, I was involved with a group of people that used to set personal goals. One of my personal goals was to spend four hours a day with God starting at four in the morning. Sounds really good and really holy right? Wrong. I am amazed at how little fruit was produced during that time. Sometimes, I would hang my head upside down and do all sorts of stuff to keep myself awake. Now, if I had been called to do this, it would have made a difference. I thought if I followed the same formula Martin Luther did, then surely my life would be as dynamic as his and I would be able to change the world for Jesus. That was his call. I learned at that point in my life, it was not mine. I had to find out things others are called to may not be mine. I was already spending deep, warm hours with God every day. Then, I put myself into this season where I prayed but nothing happened because I was not willing to relax and enjoy Him. My relationship was fun, but I ignored it because it did not look like Martin Luther's. I lost my rest and as a result, I lost my peace. When I lose my peace, I pay way too high of a price.

Once my peace was restored, I was able to have fun once again. In case you have not noticed, I love fun. I love to express myself to God in an engaging manner. What I don't enjoy is forcing myself to stay awake so I can look good, believing I will receive brownie points. I no longer strive toward the all-knowing pinnacle, believing what I do will look good in heaven. The relationship I have with Christ now and the tenderness that exists are not worth sabotaging for something I think needs to happen.

My relationship with God was sweet and tender before I took up what I thought it was supposed to look like. I have never been Martin Luther. It was senseless to think my relationship was to look like his. What I am able to do is crawl up in what seems to be Father's lap and share my heart with Him and listen to His. Those intimate talks are so necessary. During those times, He exchanges all that I am for all that He is. Without this realization that my relationship is enough right where it was and where it was going, I would always compare what I do with what others do. Comparison causes me to discount who He is and where He wants to lead me.

Father is so very kind to us in so many ways. If we feel the call to get up at whatever time, then I am sure He sees that as a wonderful sacrifice. It's important that we bring everything to Him with joy. I found myself feeling bogged down because I wanted a goal. But the goal was not birthed out of my relationship with God. It was birthed out of my need to look good and become spiritually astute via works.

Many years ago, I was in a pain center for an injury I had experienced in a car accident. The center took on every part of my life, including my marriage. It was here that I talked about how my marriage was not working. I was led to confess that I watched sometimes four hours a day of soap operas. I had watched them from a young age. They were what taught me what marriage and romance was supposed to be. The woman whom I talked with challenged me when she insisted that asking my husband to live up to those standards was probably not fair to him, nor was it fair to me. I began to release my husband to be who he was and not some Hollywood image that did not work for us.

In looking back over the years, not only did I demand of myself to be involved in cookie cutter religion, I also demanded many others, including my family, fit in a cookie cutter mold as well. This always damaged relationships and did not allow the freedom we have in Christ. I believed if my husband was a man of God, he would treat me like a romance story. I believed if I was truly spiritual, I would get up early in the morning and spend many hours praying while others slept. I'm not saying husbands aren't to cherish their wives. However, when I compared my husband to Hollywood romance, I missed his type of romance. When I choose someone else's relationship with Christ, I have no value for my own.

CHAPTER 16 FIVE POINTS TO THE CHANGE PROCESS

#1 DECIDING GOD IS FUN

If fun was a how to, this book would have been four paragraphs, maybe shorter. Fun is not a how to. It is a choice, a decision, an attitude. It's not something that is present outside of you. It's something you set your mind to. Deciding God is fun is just the beginning. To see that He portrays Himself as fun in scripture is a good start. If God had not been fun, would Moses have been up on the mountain so long? I can't imagine He would have spent forty days on a mountain with a boring God. The time God took to show Moses the mysteries of Himself must have been amazing. If I had been Moses, I would have looked into the cloud with excitement and fear, wondering what would happen next. Moses never said (at least that we know of), "Not today, God, I have too much to do to entertain your company."

If you believe God is fun, you will begin to see your life as an amazing adventure of excitement and delight. There will be moments when things are not always so blissful. While there may be more than a few of these moments, you will also learn to move through them quicker because you will adapt to what He is telling you and not what is keeping you in a difficult way of thinking.

#2 DECISION POINT

I have noticed with every situation I have a decision point. I feel Holy Spirit saying to me, "What are you going to do? What are you going to believe?" It's the same question all the time. One yes to Him in the moment. Then, it's another yes in another moment. He's so very gracious to me. If it takes me a while to figure it out, He sends me a movie or something that will get my attention to what He is attempting to say to me. My understanding of the change He offers is that it comes at these decision points.

Recently, I watched a movie about God supplying all my needs. It was a good movie and the Lord reminded me how I had gotten lost in worry over finances. Something I had been doing for a while. What a nasty habit that is, this thing called worry. As a result, He addressed all my doubt. I am so grateful we look at these things together and that I no longer need to feel as if I am on my own.

#3 DEPENDENCE

It's obvious to me I'm still quite rule oriented. Thus, I want regulations to run my life. When it comes to driving a car, that works. However, when it comes to God, regulations often take Him out of the equation as I move towards doing things for Him as opposed to doing things with Him. When I do it for Him, not with Him, once again I am adhering to the law and ignoring that in all things I have help.

Jesus put it this way:

"Not everyone who says to Me, 'Lord, Lord,' shall enter the kingdom of heaven, but He who does the will of My Father in heaven. Many will say to Me in that day, 'Lord, Lord, have we not prophesied in Your name, cast out demons in Your name, and done many wonders in Your name?' And then I will declare to them, 'I never knew you; depart from Me, you who practice lawlessness'" (Matthew 7: 22-24).

So, what might the difference be in doing it for Him versus doing it with Him? Well, when doing anything with Him, I am cooperating with Him and doing it His way, which has much greater fruit. When I do it for Him, I am following some rule or plan where I am primarily the one in charge, not giving heed to His step by step instruction. I am the one in control, not the one dependent upon the relationship I have with Him.

There are multiple examples of this. God told Abraham he would have a son. Abraham didn't wait for God's timing. His wife stepped in and he did not argue. He left God's plan behind, thinking all it took was a sperm and an egg to bring forth a child of promise. That decision gave them years of misery and yet, God still gave him a son of promise. It just came out of what they thought was impossible.

I love giving words to people about how God feels about them and what He is thinking about them. It has not always been that way. When I first started giving words to people in public places, I did it as one who was told what to tell them by God. Often, I felt like I was being shoved out the door. Not by God, that attitude came from within. I found myself anxious, frustrated and afraid a lot of the time.

As I began to relax and decide that God was bigger than my fear of how I looked to a stranger, things eventually shifted for me. I began to tell people what I heard as I stood having a conversation with Holy Spirit in my head. I learned I was not alone. I also learned God really loves people and wants to encourage them in their everyday lives. I changed as He showed me how to change. I always wanted this kind of change and He purposed it and brought me to it. I could have never formulated this plan on my own.

#4 Realizing and choosing to believe He is for us
When it came to looking at things through a new light, I had to learn I was not alone. I learned I no longer had to fight to see things through the lens of fun. I only had to acknowledge that He was there with me and He was more than willing to help me achieve what we both wanted. When I struggled with negative thoughts I thought about how they detoured my mood causing me to feel gloomy. I did not like being gloomy any more than the next person. In this, I would take a look at my thoughts and decide if I liked the way I was thinking or if the mood I was experiencing was something I wanted to change.

#5 This is a process
I found out I could not change my thoughts by panicking. If anything, that made the negative thoughts more persistent. I learned one of the first things I had to do was to ask God for the grace to accept who I was in that moment. If I did not accept who I was, then I was telling myself I was not okay and that was an impossible position to change my thoughts from. When I gave in to accepting myself as wonderfully imperfect and became okay with what I was thinking, it was as if I was able to really look at my thoughts without judgement and decide which ones could stay and which ones could leave. I also knew I was not alone in this process because Holy Spirit and I would have a lot of discussion around this.

I love Holy Spirit. He makes this process so amazing. He's the first to inquire, "Is this what you want to be thinking?" He always asks me without judgement, with choice and with the door open for me to step through into the power to stop any thought I no longer want to think. All I have to do is say help, and I am given what I need to move beyond that present thought. His help moves me there more quickly than I could ever move myself in my own strength.

My thought life has been a progression of training by Holy Spirit. In my early career as a people helper, I worked for a sexual assault center answering crisis calls. From that job, I learned a very valuable life lesson. Not everything I hear needs to become a picture in my mind. The stories were unfortunate. I did not want those images in my head. I knew if I kept allowing my imagination to attach pictures to the words I heard I would burn out quickly. I showed empathy and addressed what I could, but I would not let my mind create pictures of their stories. This allowed me to remain fresh in my job and not become unduly burdened.

I remember these slide shows I used to watch in Sunday school as a child. In one, Martin Luther quoted a hermit saying to a young man who was being tempted by sin, "You can't stop the birds from flying over your head, but only let them fly. Don't let them nest in your hair." That is how I feel about negative thoughts. I am learning more and more to let them fly. Some, I'm learning to not even allow entry into my airspace. This has become a long process. I am not alone in it as Holy Spirit has been quite faithful.

Chapter 17 Fruit

What kind of Christian will others perceive us to be if we are having fun? That is a really good question. Being a fun Christian is about being what Jesus told us we were — salt and light. Jesus declared we are "the light of the world" and "the salt of the earth." If we are not having fun how could we ever bring light into every situation? How could we ever be the flavor every situation so desperately needs?

I hear people talk about hypocrites a lot when they talk about the church. I think that is because a lot of people outside the church see miserable people trying to live a life that is impossible to live. When we embrace God, we embrace His perfection, not our own. Our own perfection (which is impossible) leads us down a road that is filled with speed bumps, potholes, wash outs and sinkholes. Jesus really did die to release us from the law. The book of Romans has this stellar announcement:

"There is therefore no condemnation for those who are in Christ Jesus, that walk not according to the flesh, but according to the spirit. For the law of the spirit of life in Christ Jesus has set me free from the law of sin and death (Romans 8:1-2, NKJV)."

I think if we really began to take this seriously, we would have a totally different experience. I think we would begin to say, "Hey, being a Christian isn't about our failings and trying to make up for them, it's about Jesus and what He is doing in me." Maybe we could switch our focus from incomplete selves onto Him. Then, we would see something worth looking at. We would see a life filled with fun and the ability to live abundantly. It will never be about what we do or don't do as long as we live this life wide open with Him.

Do you think if people see us having fun as Christians they might actually see a life they want? It may offend some, even as Jesus offended the Pharisees. He also welcomed many who needed him. He welcomed them to the places He stayed. Jesus loved to go to the parties of the day, or so I would presume by how many He went to that were recorded in the Bible. The accusations of the religious people of the day did not stop Jesus. He hung out with sinners. Obviously, He enjoyed himself or why would He have done it so much? Unless, we want to pin on Him that 'it was his mission field.' Please, give me a break. If Jesus had not loved the people He was with and loved being with them, how would Zacchaeus exclaiming that he would repay all that he had stolen and give half of what he did have to the poor have ever happened. This was the result of a party not sanctioned by the religious people.

CHAPTER 18 MORE FRUIT

Some people in my life hate what one might call Christian Disciplines. That is because they are thinking from a religious mindset. They believe the victim Christian line, "I have to do it." Please allow me to free you. No, you don't have to do it. But, let's look at it again from a different perspective.

I began to think about things a long time ago in a different way. I came to a place where I did not want to be a victim in any part of my life. This can make me a lot of work to be around, for sure. I guess I believe Jesus died so I could be free not sentenced to a life of religious servitude. So many Christians aren't having fun because they live within a religious prison. They feel they have to pray over and over to move the hand of God. They have to read their Bible. They have to go to church and they have to…. (fill in the blank because there is about a million of them). I changed it all when I changed my wording and my mind set. I went from "I have to . . ." to "I get to. . ." which is about choice and love.

Growing up in a system where control was the rule, I always thought doing the things Christian's do was heavy and difficult. I really understood what Jesus said when He took on the Pharisees. I was one and I had become one through obeying my own law of having to. Now, I spend my time wanting to.

At thirteen, after making a promise to do so at a conference I attended, I began nightly Bible readings on a regular basis. I would not have been able to tell you what I read after I finished. In those days, I read *The Living Bible.* Half awake, I read one chapter religiously every night before I went to bed. I was doing it though and I figured I was getting points in heaven because of it. I remember if I did not do it something bad would happen. It became a superstitious act for me. *Again, I was somehow earning God's love by my faithfulness instead of receiving his love because He is faithful.*

Now, I read my Bible with an 'I want to.' What do You have for me today, Father? What amazing revelation are You going to show me? What will I find out about You in your letter to me today? My attitude changed it all. I changed me, not my time, not my Bible (although I do read all different translations, depending on what seems to speak to me at the moment), not God. I changed my way of looking at it. Right now, I have my phone read it to me and I love it. If I need to go back and study something I'm drawn to, I will. I love the Word washing over me as it is read from an app on my phone. Bible reading is wonderful when I come at it with an 'I want to' thought process.

There are so many fun possibilities in Bible reading. So many of us were programed to trudge our way through it painfully with the reading of it being the goal. When I first started reading the Bible with fun in mind, I began to look at the people and their relationship with God. I wanted to know what Moses was really thinking. I would put myself back there. Would I have been enamored with the cloud by day and the fire by night or would I have thought that was normal? Would my heart be compelled like Joshua's to desire to stay in the tent or on the mountain when God was there no matter the cost or would I have been too busy paying attention to other things? I still wonder that about myself. Am I focusing on the cloud of His presence in my life or am I too busy with other parts of life to notice? This is a fun question for me. I like the challenge of paying attention to what is going on. If I'm not paying attention, then I am missing it.

What the Bible teaches me is thrilling. I can change my course when I have revelation and that is fun too. It's not fun merely living in busy instead of the relationship we have been given with God.

Reading the Bible can also not be fun if we spend all our time reading it and deciding that we do not measure up. When we judge ourselves, we make our life difficult. Essentially, we are telling God He does not know how to disciple us and we become the makers of ourselves. This is probably how the self-made man originated. When we are self-made, we have to push ourselves into places and demand perfection (there is that word again) from ourselves. When we read the Bible looking for the fun in it, we find that measuring up is not the end all. With the exception of Jesus, no one in the Bible measured up to perfection. Not Moses, not

Abraham, and certainly not Adam. Knowing that makes it possible to put our minds at ease and hook up to Jesus. It is here that we can look, not to our weaknesses, but to His love that will transform us. You can't transform yourself except to demand from the flesh and the fruit of the flesh is putrid.

When David wrote:

"Your word is a lamp to my feet and a light to my path" (Psalm 119:105).

He was declaring that God's word had the ability to guide the direction in the way he was to go. He knew there was promise in the word of God that he could not do without. He knew the power in it. Most likely by this time, he had experienced it over and over in his life. The Word of God is truth for more than David, for us as well.

CHAPTER 19 MORE AND MORE FRUIT

Pray without Ceasing (I Thessalonians 5:17)

Paul said these words and I gather he found prayer very delightful. He knew prayer is just a conversation with God. I love having those conversations with God all day long. Often they are about what I am feeling. Sometimes, they are about what I am thinking. I talk and sometimes He corrects and sometimes He just listens. I know He listens because that is what He does. He is never too busy to listen. He enjoys our company, or so I would gather. He has put so much value on us, to think otherwise is contrary to what we see in this loving Father.

Jesus showed us the Lord's Prayer as a light into talking and asking. In prayer, I get to talk, worship and ask. I ask other people in my life for things so why would I not ask God. I'm also committed to the idea that God wants us to ask.

Jesus said, "Ask, and it will be given to you. Seek, and you will find. Knock, and the door will be open to you."

"If you being evil give good things to your children, how much more will your heavenly father give to those who ask" (Luke 11:13, NKJV).

Again, we are given permission to ask. This is an opportunity to talk to God and have a conversation about what we want and need.

The hard part about prayer, oftentimes, is that it puts us in a place of vulnerability. Most people don't like being vulnerable. When I share with God what I want and need, I am opening up my heart to Him and allowing Him to see the desires of my heart. This can present a problem for some.

Years ago, we had people over to our house for nightly meetings on a regular basis. I used to pull out a chair for them and a chair for God. Few could sit in that chair with the idea of God sitting there talking to them. It was difficult because who they thought God was in their mind somehow made them afraid of being that close to Him. I still encourage people to do this exercise. It's a practice of conversation with a God that is close and not distant. When we allow God to have a close relationship with us, we find Him willing to come in and be intimate with us.

If the idea of having a close relationship with God seems difficult to you, you may want to ask yourself what makes it difficult. You may have to ask several questions and acknowledge the uncomfortable answers. If it is because you feel you don't measure up, Jesus made a way for that. He is already committed to you knowing his love. If you think it's because God does not measure up, talk to Him about that. Talk to Him about your disappointments. Talk to Him about your fears. Talk to Him about how you think He is something other than the Bible says He is. You may not get all the answers you are looking for. However, when you start the discussion you are on a new road to fun.

I have a group of friends that has been a part of my life for ten years. In this time, we have been praying for people to come to Christ. It has been a time of praying for nations and praying for people and praying for one another. It has been fruitful and it has had moments of conflict. We have been very aware of each other's lives with the ups and downs. We live in three or four different states (varies with who is on our call). We meet on the phone every morning unless we don't want to. There is no demand to be on and there is no pressure to be on. We love each other. That is part of the joy of doing this. We find pleasure in our time. Sometimes we discuss things going on with us and sometimes we just pray. Ten years ago when Father asked me to do this, I never dreamed it would go on this long. These are now long term relationships and they are people I trust with my life. These relationships God has knit together over time and with great care and are very dear to me. I am grateful for them and that to me is exciting.

Prayer is an adventure, an extension of our amazing relationship. It's a heart to heart connection in conversation that yields to a great desire for Him.

Chapter 20 Living Excited

I refuse the life of a victim. I'm excited about every moment of this life. Every moment is filled with anticipation, as if something wonderful is about to happen. That is what fun with God is like. Continuous expectation of Him doing something I have not experienced before or a new twist on something I have. Each moment has this amazing flavor. It's a life of expectation.

Here is my internal narrative to Him:

"This life of You, my God, asking and me saying yes. Or, me asking and You, My Father, saying okay, let's go. It's breaking through me to get to You. It's finding that there is this huge moment of great awareness. You are beyond my wildest dreams and that is exactly what You want to be to me. You want to be beyond my wildest. You desire to give me this amazing life that has more fun in it with each moment than I ever dreamed. The only thing that would ever keep me from having fun in the next minute is things that have kept me from having fun in the past, and I'm tired of living that life. I want this life of looking for You, of discovering what You are doing, as if You sneak up on me and pull my pigtail while I giggle with the surprise, and sheer delight, of a little child being thrown into the beauty of You. You are the spring in my step, the dew on my lips and the laughter in my heart. You are way beyond my imagination. To break through to get to You is what I want every minute of my life, because while I say I am getting through to You, the truth is You are the one opening the door and pulling me through and that is what You want."

God and I are working on renewing my mind at a pretty fast pace right now. It's what we want to do and I do it with joy. I am also finding it so much fun. I can hardly keep from giggling all the time. I've found that in the process, Holy Spirit is having a lot of fun as well. He is so good at helping me through this change. The question, "do you really want to do that?" comes up all the time. I hear the smile on His face. No longer do my filters perceive judgement in His voice. Continually, I am reminded:

"Or do you show contempt for the riches of his kindness, forbearance and patience, not realizing that God's kindness is intended to lead you to repentance" (Romans 2:4, NIV)?

Isn't that cool? It's not His judgmental attitude. It's His kindness that draws us to Him because of our need for it. So, in this process I tell Him what I really think, and we have this love fest. It is so fun.

PART IV BOOSTERS

Chapter 21   Fun Boosters

So what makes this relationship with Father so fun? I have learned to accept certain things within our relationship that tend to open up new possibilities and release any hindrance. These are suggestions that have worked for me. By no means make a law out of them. We are so good at saying, "Well, this has not happened because you have not done this or because you have done that." This will not work. I suggest you pray about these things before you decide if you are able to accept them. As you start praying, realize how delightful it is to pray and enjoy the moment with Him.

In showing me these things, Holy Spirit has helped me look at life differently. If you decide to accept them, most likely you will find yourself in the fun zone more frequently. It's not something you have to do. It's actually something you can accept. And, while you may struggle with accepting it at first, you will also find that in the midst of the acceptance everything will transform. Though we often want everything to remain the same, these are powerful to accept if you decide to. There is always more to the experience.

Take going on a trip to Italy for example. I can go to Rome, but if I never visit the Colosseum, I will be missing part of the fun of Rome. If I never have pizza, I will miss part of the experience of Rome. If I never talk to the people that live there, if I never go to Florence or have gelato, I will miss out on part of the understanding of Italy. If I never tour Venice or fail to see San Marco Plaza, I will be missing out on a great piece of Italy. I'm sure by now you get the idea. This is about accepting the things that add to the overall depth of your relationship with Jesus. As you accept these things, you will find yourself feeling surer of yourself and that is of course – fun.

Take these as things to accept, not in their entirety, but as decrees in the first line. You are in process. Address the "I accept" and allow your brain and heart to grab it knowing your spirit will run with it.

CHAPTER 22 BOOSTER #1

I ACCEPT MY LIFE IS A LIFE OF BEING WELL LOVED BY HIM.

I accept that His love does not demand from me what I cannot give.

The idea of His love making up the difference took me a long time to learn. For years, my Christian walk was works based because I had so little revelation of grace, love and rest. I used to think I had to be a particular type of person to not bring shame to Jesus. I thought the whole world was watching me and that somehow it was important that I put on a Christian face. The amazing thing was when I slipped, my slips were so horrendous. I felt such shame, as if all Jesus had done on the cross could not take care of the mistakes I made. It was living in bondage at its best. There was no freedom and little hope.

I am no longer expected to live by the law. I would be unable to fulfill the law even if I did attempt to live by it. The law has been fulfilled once and for all and it is no longer necessary for me to be my own savior. Jesus, who is so fun, so amazing and so wonderful, has paid the price not just for my sin, but also for my rest.

Now I know that His love for me is no longer a burden. It allows me to live in such freedom that I don't have to worry about not being who I think He wants me to be. I am released to be a new creation. One who is free to emulate Christ, not because of what I do, but because of who is living in me. I am now free to be whole because that is where He has placed me. He did not place me in work and toil. He placed me in love. He placed me into His righteousness. He placed me in His heart where I am forever held because of who He is, not because of who I am.

When I think about His love for me and how He is excited to cover me in it, I become so very impressed with who He is. I keep thinking that He is doing something so beyond my understanding – and He is. All He asks of me is to accept it. For me, saying yes to His love is to say yes to a lifetime of freedom. In accepting that this life is one of love, I accept that I am accepted to the praise of the glory of His grace, by which He made us accepted in the Beloved (Ephesians 1:6, NKJV).

What does it mean to you to be accepted by God and therefore accepted into Christ? What does that mean when you are called into that place and you are able to know that you know that you are loved? How does that alter your life? How does that change who you are? How does that revolutionize your very DNA in your thinking? Be aware that you can change your DNA by your thoughts. So, what happens if you begin to believe that you were meant for love, that you were meant to be loved, to accept love and to allow love to flow through you as if you were a water pipe? That's an exciting thought! Maybe you can be a fire hydrant and let love flow through you at that magnitude. I have been around a few people who were like that and I was amazed when I saw it. Maybe that is you. I know I want it to be me as well.

What will the world be like when we realize we were meant to have love flow through us as though we were fire hydrants? What kind of joy will we have flowing out of our bellies when we realize if we quit worrying about who we are not? How much love will we allow to spill out when we realize who He is? I know there was a time in my life when I probably did not release any more water than a leaky faucet. Now that I think about it, that was pretty boring too. The idea of being a fire hydrant is much more fun. In being a fire hydrant, you could put out the fire of pain in someone's life. If we are a major waterfall, we could bring hope to a parched city. When we grab this revelation and realize how amazing He is and how much He really wants us to walk with Him, everything will change. We will see the most amazing things being done on the earth. And it will be about Him, as we will know how helpless we would be to do it on our own. That level of cooperation with Him would be fun.

David said,

"Where can I go from Your Spirit? Or where can I flee from Your presence" (Psalm 139:7, NKJV)?

He had it right. He really did. He knew nothing could separate Him from God. He was so aware of the presence of God. He was convinced God was so close that He could not get away from Him.

Paul addressed it another way.

"For I am persuaded that neither death nor life, nor angels nor principalities nor powers, nor things present nor things to come, nor height nor depth, nor any other created thing, shall be able to separate us from the love of God which is in Christ Jesus our Lord" (Romans 8:38-39, NKJV).

That is truth. Nothing can separate us from His love. If the same God who sent His son to pay the price for me is committed to loving me, who am I to stop Him? I could not, anyway. There is no way to stop Him. He is the greatest of all lovers, forever determined not to withdraw His love but to press on in loving even the unlovable.

I accept God accepts me in this process and uses it all and I can trust that.

I used to think His love was conditional and that what I had done in the past had certainly put a problem between Him and me. I repented twenty-two years for something I thought I had done wrong. It was not clear sin. It was a problem with perspective, on my part. I felt I had chosen to move in a different direction than what God had for me. One day I was doing my usual lamenting/repenting and He stopped me and very loudly said, "I always intended for that to happen." At first, I was a little irritated thinking He could have let me know that twenty-one years ago. I also realized He had not withdrawn his love during that time, neither did He see it as the end of the world as I had played it out in my mind. He had actually been in my future and had seen how much hope and growth had happened as a result of that particular decision.

During the repentant time, I really did believe I was walking in some sort of diminished level of His love. I believed I was a lesser person. I felt less saved because I thought my decision was different than His. His love alone is the equalizer for all of us. It's what brings us in to a place of acceptance.

I look at the word of God and I don't see a diminished level of love from God anywhere. I see Him take people who are broken and do the unexpected with them. I see Him looking for ways to make them spectacular because of who He is.

Take the adopted Hebrew who led millions out of Egypt into the wilderness. I am sure Moses was never loved in a diminished capacity. He lived in Pharaoh's courts before he murdered someone. Nor was there a minor love offered to him after he disobeyed God and received an early death. God sets the rules and makes the play, but a smaller portion of love is not in the playbook. To those who want it, there is always a heart wide open waiting to take them in.

Take the shepherd boy who killed a giant. He messed up after being a king for many years. His fear was that God would take His Holy Spirit from him. What a fear. Yet, we see elsewhere that God's love persisted in David's life. We see God doing all sorts of mighty acts for Judah, for "My servant David's sake." God never quits loving us ever.

Then, there was Paul. He didn't like Christians. God loved Him and His heart had to express itself to Paul in a way that knocked him off his horse. He would never be the same. Up to that point, he knew of God through the law. God turned the tables on him, showing him His love. He also gave Paul a mission, which with Paul's personality, was important because I would imagine Paul always wanted something to do. He had gone to the council to seek out and destroy the church. God gave Paul an amazing assignment. Instead of Paul hunting men down, he became a fisher of men. I guess he was a sportsman, anyway you look at it. Now, his bait was the love of Christ which he could not be separated from.

CHAPTER 23 BOOSTER #2 I ACCEPT THAT I AM A PRIEST AND A KING TO MY GOD.

"And from Jesus Christ, the faithful witness, the firstborn from the dead, and the ruler over the kings of the earth. To Him who loved us and washed us from our sins in His own blood, and has made us kings and priests to His God and Father, to Him be glory and dominion forever and ever. Amen" (Revelation 1:6-7, NKJV).

I am a priest and so are you. Hmm, I have wondered about what that means often in this present day. The priest of the past took care of the people's spiritual needs and administered the sacrifice in the temple. The need for a sacrifice has been taken care of by our great High Priest, so we no longer need to worry about that (yeah!). So, what does it mean for us to be a priest?

In many ways, being a priest says we are no longer a second class citizen. We are the ones in service before the Lord. We are also responsible for our own feeding. This may sound a little sacrilegious, but please bear with me.

We are now the priests of our own lives. We no longer have to have someone else give us spiritual food. We are able to come to God and eat from His hand, delight in His presence and not have to wait for someone else to hear Him for us. We no longer have to believe that someone else must tell us what to do. We are told to come boldly before the throne of grace. What does that mean? To not worry about whether or not we are welcomed because we are.

The priest who entered the Holy of Holies once a year at Passover had to be careful. He had all these laws to follow and everything was required to be just right. He even had a rope tied around his ankle in case He died while behind the veil. We aren't those kinds of priests because the curtain has been torn. The tearing of the curtain makes Him available to us. We can go and eat from His table and hear what is on His heart. Not by doing something of the law, but by believing we can and watching Him draw closer than we ever could. It really is all about Him.

He has given me access to minister to Him, even as a priest does. So, what does ministering to God mean at this time since it is no longer about following the law? Well, Jesus is our High Priest. We have His example, which is the best of all. Jesus, being High Priest spends time with Father even now. So, our priest life is also about spending time with God. It really is that easy. Our priestly duty to God is to be with Him, to love Him and find that whatever He asks us to do is fun because we can trust Him. We really will have to make the decision as to whether it is fun or not. It is a choice. When we choose that our priestly relationship is fun, it becomes so free and refreshing. Otherwise, all we have is painful, boring religion, and we become an Old Testament priest, worried about our life if we go behind the veil.

But we aren't just priests, we are also kings. Nothing, and I mean nothing, is like the awareness of being royalty. Don't you love that? You're a king. Not a queen, because this is not about gender. Queens are only given access to the throne if there aren't any male heirs that qualify. No, you are a king. Not just any king, you're a king under the King of kings. So, what does it mean to be a King? Good question.

A king is raised to know who he is. He is raised with the idea that he is a ruler that is compassionate and able to hold the line over his kingdom when necessary. He is diplomatic with other kings and is willing to do what is best for his kingdom. A king that knows he is a servant is the wisest of all. He is not easily threatened by the growth of others, but encourages it. He is kind and benevolent, and willing to take the necessary risks to grow his kingdom. A king that does not know these things starts unnecessary wars and may even be a tyrant.

How do you relate to being a king? Where are you a king in your own life? Have you taken up being a king at work? Do you see yourself as placed there for important reasons, to pray and to serve and to love those you work with? Or, do you see yourself as one that survives the days and really does not care much for those around you unless they act like you and think like you?

I have learned when I decide to serve and to love those I work with, I show up as a king in the workplace. I pray for the place and I see changes within a few months that make the most amazing difference in the jobs I do. The beautiful thing is, I also transform in this process because I learned a secret. I don't have to continue to be miserable. I learned I can choose to be a king and watch everything around me adjust to the kingdom of light. I learned I can have joy in the midst of great pain where people are struggling. I learned I can love people I do not completely understand, even those who before may have been difficult to love. I also learned a king has another's best interest in mind, not just his own. The most loving thing I could do was bring in a different choice besides my previous attitude. I became the servant and the king.

I accept that I have access to the Father.

Sometimes I am so amazed at how many Christians believe they do not have direct access to God. I often meet people who have fire insurance and don't know what to do after that. It's amazing to me how I believe so differently from so many people. There are many who believe God may or may not hear their prayers. Some believe He hears, but question if He cares. Others feel God is more aloof. I'm reminded of lyrics from a Bette Midler song, "God is watching us from a distance." I remember when I first heard the song. I thought, "I don't think so."

That is one of the things I find really fun about God. He is so involved in our lives. He is waiting to be included and He wants to be involved. We, on the other hand, seldom know what to do with a God who waits for us with arms wide open. I think we are so afraid that if we actually get a glimpse of Him, we will see all that is bad about ourselves. And that might be true, but that is the reason He presented a plan of salvation. Not so we could feel bad about ourselves all the time, but so we could feel really good about Him and His love for us.

If I want to stare at my sin, my past, all my wounds and all the places I have messed up, there really is no end to it. However, if I turn my gaze to Him, all His splendor, majesty and beauty, there is no end to that. I believe staring at Him actually addresses all my stuff and changes things inside of me.

When I am afraid, I usually hide because I am staring at all my imperfections. In those instances, I am choosing to bring myself into the place of believing I am inadequate and unable to do anything right. How can that be true with Christ living in me?

"I can do all things through Christ who strengthens me" (Phil 4:13, NKJV).

His living in me makes all things possible. His love breaks all the barriers I have erected that built a wall between Him and I. It is encouraging that I only need to look up and see that He has removed the veil. He is there. I see Him, just Him, smiling at me with a hug on His arms waiting for me to receive it. He really does love us beyond our sin, pain and rebellion. And, if we think we don't like our sin, that is nothing compared to how He feels about it considering He is so very wonderfully holy. Yet, it is His holiness that works to mend us and make us so He can shine in the most beautiful way through us. That was always His plan. It was not to condemn us but to encourage us to live wide open. When we choose to live with all that we are in a given moment, it is then we have relationship. We have communion. We have a place where we are safe and well held. We are His children. We have access to the most precious of all relationships in the universe. We have access to Him as we meet Him in all of life.

CHAPTER 24 BOOSTER #3

I ACCEPT THAT I AM A WARRIOR OF LIGHT IN A BATTLE WITH DARKNESS.

I have learned warfare is exciting. Oh, I know that sounds crazy, but it is fun. For me, it is delightful waking up every morning knowing today is another day the enemy will be defeated wherever I walk. Sounds arrogant? Maybe. But, then if Christ lives in me, is that not part of my purpose, even as He destroys the works of the enemy. Remember, no matter what, we win.

While I will have setbacks, they will only make me stronger and more resolute to what He has for me. I know God will give me all I need to defeat the enemy in my life. The bonus is that in following Him, I also get to help others defeat the enemy in their lives. It's amazing what a warrior of light can do.

Being a warrior of light brings about promise. Sometimes, it will be my promises and sometimes other people's promises depending on what is being fought for. I get to walk into darkness and declare, by my very presence, that darkness' time is done and that light will invade the darkness because of Christ in me. Remember this verse,

"You are of God, little children, and have overcome them, because He who is in you is greater than He who is in the world "(1 John 4:4, NKJV).

John reminds us that Christ in us is greater than the enemy. He tells us that we have overcome him. Just because it does not feel like it does not make it truth. Jesus living in you is so ginormous, the enemy fears you and what you can do to his kingdom. If you want to choose a kingdom on which to wage war, choose that one. Of course, in case you have not figured it out, you are already at war with the enemy. It's how you fight it that will make the difference. When you fight it from the relationship where you are becoming molded into the image of Christ, anything you do or become will be a swipe at the enemy, and you will not even realize it.

I have had the opportunity to pray in unusual places all over the world. One of my favorite places to pray is the commuter trains. In many countries I have visited, I look around and see there are most likely no believers on the train. I think wow, what a great opportunity to pray into and release what God has planned for that area. I begin to pray for salvation for those on the commuter train. Some people who are prayer people may never see their faces, but I can, and I enjoy silently praying for them. I always pray in faith with the idea that they may not know who He is now, but that will not last for long. I know God is always up to something. In that moment, I am with Him and He is with me and things are bound to change.

The thing I am most aware of as a warrior of light is that the battle is already won. That is so right. The battle is already done, won and the enemy is on the run. I believe I have a powerful presence inside of me that makes the enemy very concerned when I show up. It is from here that I can live in the idea that the enemy is a goner. He is without hope because the God of hope has already declared him defeated.

Since the battle is the Lord's, who has already defeated the enemy, then it is done. I am light and God is light. He abides in me, what more could I ask for. He's determined to show me how great a God He is. All I have to do is come to the party. He's going to defeat the enemy showing me how awesome and how powerful He is. All I have to do is say yes.

The thing to remember is there is no longer a reason for us to be afraid. If the battle is the Lord's, then it really is His. We must go forward and trust that He truly does have it all under His timing and power.

I accept that the same power that raised Christ from the dead lives in me.

I'm pretty sure those are Paul's words, not mine.

"But if the Spirit of Him who raised Jesus from the dead dwells in you, He who raised Christ from the dead will also give life to your mortal bodies through His Spirit who dwells in you" (Romans 8: 11, NKJV).

Is that just about being raised from the dead or is it about something more?

When we became born again, we accepted the new life of the Holy Spirit to live in us. Have you ever thought about what that really means? Have you ever thought about the fact that the living God has chosen to take up residence in you? The Creator of the universe has declared that since you've asked, He will make His home in you. That is amazing and mind blowing, in a fun way. I love the fact that He decided to do this. I love that He chose to take residence inside of me.

What does that mean to me? To be honest, I don't always know. I would like to be able to wrap my mind completely around this one, but then I go back to the "eyes have not seen..." verse and I am adrift in amazement because I have so little idea of what it means. All I know is, it is a fact. A fact He has declared because I said, "Yes." Or maybe I screamed it. I'm not always quite sure.

I am committed to the idea that He limits himself within me until I am ready to completely say yes to what He wants to do next. He wants my full cooperation. Without it, I'm a whiner. Sometimes, I ask Him to do these changes in me and to continue even if I whine. I'm learning that my whining is boring and silly. Often, I laugh at myself and my own predictability because honestly, He is giving me exactly what I have been asking for. What my heart has been crying for He says yes to. Then, He stretches me so I can hold it all. A lot more of His power in my life so He can do above and beyond all that I can ask and think. How amazing is that?

So, what is this power that raised Christ from the dead doing inside of me? Well, what it is doing inside of me is messing with my head all the time and putting a smile on my face because of it. It's telling me of adventures, of His great love, of how He wants me to be closer to Him than I ever imagined and that He will tell me great things in the night season and talk to me in the day time. He always tells me there is more to learn and I will get it all because of His commitment, not necessarily mine.

The nice thing about Him is He knows who I am and He is not concerned about how far I fall from perfection. I worry that I will miss it. He has already been there to make sure I get it. There is no worry on His part. He knows my frame. He's always seen it and He has always loved it.

I accept that when all may appear hopeless, God will bring in hope.

I am not sure there is a worse feeling than feeling hopeless. People who are hopeless live in depression and despair. It's an effect of being lost in one's own belief that stems from being let down continuously. I should know. I have been there. I remember one moment when I was feeling hopeless. It had been a difficult year in our home. I wondered when it would end. I did not realize I had allowed the enemy (yes allowed) to pick at me all the time. The enemy was not going away because I had not chosen a different way to look at things. God began to speak to me that I had given away my hope and He was determined to restore it. After He spoke to me, I began to look at things differently. I had been the one that walked away from hope. I decided to choose hope to be my word for a season. After that, I looked for hope everywhere.

Most of us know what the absence of hope looks like and what it feels like. It feels horrible, like nothing is right. Like nothing will be right. It feels like we will be stuck forever, as if there is no way out. It feels like self-pity, like everyone else is doing better and getting more than us. Hopeless people are the poor victims of the moment who often feel as if they don't have a choice as to where they are in life.

What a difficult place to be. I felt like this much of my life when I trusted more in religious activity than I did in this amazing God I'm in love with. Religious activity was drying my bones. I always felt weary and hopeless. I thought it would take forever for me to finally please God. Figuring out He is not that way is a gift.

With a clearer understanding of what no hope feels like, let's examine the converse. What does hope feel like? Hope feels like sparkling clear water on a hot day. Like a friendly smile in the midst of a crowd of unfamiliar faces. Hope feels like a cool breeze on a hot summer day. In hope, there is always promise. There is a promise that something is going to change. When we hold hope close, we become optimistic and see that delight is always around the corner, somewhere. Maybe the corner takes longer than we plan, but we know it's there. Somewhere, we will find it, and when we do, we squeal with joy. Hope is a gift from God that keeps us persevering into overcoming what we never thought would be possible. The heart is often stronger and more persistent at holding on to what has been promised.

Chapter 25 Booster #4

I accept that God's love will break through into every aspect of my life

If God is nothing else, He is persistent in His great love for us. I love that about Him. I love that His love changes everything.

"What marvelous love the Father has extended to us! Just look at it - we're called children of God! That's who we really are. But that's also why the world doesn't recognize us or take us seriously, because it has no idea who He is or what he's up to" (1 John 3:1, The Message).

This journey called life is filled with many different layers of revelation. What I find is that God will take on a particular piece of my character, then He will move on and take on another part. Then, He will address another part, as He can only address as much as I am willing to allow Him. I adore that about Him. He will only take on what I am willing to say yes to.

The scary part is when I ask Him to take on stuff in me and He actually does it. It's only scary because I say to myself, "Wow, He got to it," and then I have the fun decision as to whether or not to agree with Him about what I asked Him to do in the first place. We humans are so confused some days. We want Him to make it so we no longer do what we don't want to do and when He goes after it at our request, we find ourselves helpless. We only need to look beyond our own flesh to the One that is orchestrating it all because we asked Him to. He is so much kinder to us than we ever dreamed. He does this out of His love for us, not because He needs to make us into His son. God has no need to do that. He hears the cry of our heart to want to be like Jesus. He obliges, moving us into that place of His great love for us. It's a delight to become the image of Jesus on the earth. Even when it is painful, we move from glory to glory in the midst of painful circumstances.

I look back and say, "I am not who I was." How has being a Christian changed you? Has it allowed His love to soak deeper into you? Have you embraced that He is coming after you to love you and set you free to a life that you have yet to discover?

CHAPTER 26 BOOSTER #5

I ACCEPT THAT I AM TAKEN CARE OF.

THERE WILL ALWAYS BE PROVISION.

When I was little, people often talked about how hard they worked as adults. I lived in a culture consumed with work ethic. This quote was common in my youth,

"For even when we were with you, we gave you this rule: "If a man will not work, He shall not eat"" (2 Thessalonians 3:10, NKJV).

Paul wrote this to keep people who were trouble makers busy. -Work was a place of pride as I was growing up. Men and women considered themselves hard workers, able to take care of their families. Then something changed.

I'm not sure what it was, maybe it became easier to trust in the government for our well-being than in God. Maybe it started with social security taking care of our elders and families no longer taking care of each other. Maybe it became about a lot of things, most of which were backbones to our society we have since discarded for another way of living. Now, we live in a world full of worry that we may not be taken care of. We worry that we might not be able to get that new vehicle, or new phone or new toy. People live together until they can afford the right wedding. They wait until they can afford children. They expect the government to take care of them in their old age. The list goes on.

I remember when we were first married. There was nothing affluent about our life. It was amazing that we had anything. It was often a place of prayer to see where the next piece of furniture would show up, where the clothes for our first born were going to come from. The thrilling part is God always took care of us. As I look back, it was like living in a mystery novel. How would kids who had nothing experience provision beyond themselves? We did, all the time. When someone heard I was pregnant they gave us eight large garbage bags full of children's clothes and toys and all sorts of supplies. We had to make two trips in our Volkswagen bug because there was so much. We were amazed at the provision.

With the idea that He will always take care of us, let's look at this amazing verse in the Bible that gives us comfort in His availability to us.

Jesus said it wonderfully,

"If God gives such attention to the appearance of wildflowers - most of which are never even seen - don't you think he'll attend to you, take pride in you, do his best for you? What I'm trying to do here is to get you to relax, to not be so preoccupied with getting, so you can respond to God's giving. People who don't know God and the way He works fuss over these things, but you know both God and how He works. Steep your life in God-reality, God-initiative, God-provisions. Don't worry about missing out. You'll find all your everyday human concerns will be met" (Matthew 6: 30-33, The Message).

Paul had a similar sentiment that was brilliant as well,

"Don't fret or worry. Instead of worrying, pray. Let petitions and praises shape your worries into prayers, letting God know your concerns. Before you know it, a sense of God's wholeness, everything coming together for good, will come and settle you down. It's wonderful what happens when Christ displaces worry at the center of your life" (Philippians 4:6-7, The Message).

Jesus told us God will take care of us. Paul tells us not to worry about whether or not we will be taken care of, but to pray and know that everything will come together. These verses push us beyond our own need to take care of ourselves into a place of faith that will manage our life in a much better order than our drive to take care of ourselves.

One time I had a friend inform me she had a vision and she believed I was part of the vision. It was of a great place where we would do ministry together. I listened to what she said and then took it to Father. I wanted to know what answer He would give me.

That night, I had a dream. If I followed after my friend, I would not live out what God had called me to do. Since that time, I see how true that was. I had to trust Father for the provision of letting me know even what truth was. Knowing the right revelations in the right time is very important. It is part of the provision for our lives, to know His plan for us that works with the very desires He put in our hearts. You know the verse,

"Delight yourself also in the Lord, And He shall give you the desires of your heart" (Psalm 37:4, NKJV).

I believe He created us with those desires, and He is in totally agreement. I also believe delighting in the Lord opens up possibilities galore. So, go for it!

I accept that I am protected.

As I go back to the story about the dream that said if I followed my friend I would not fulfill my calling, I realize I am protected. I am protected by His love and grace. I know difficult things happen, many difficult things happen in a lifetime and still, in the midst of all the difficult things, we are protected from the full force of the blow of the enemy. Father does move situations around to protect us. He does move circumstances so the worst never happens. Some days it feels like it.

One day, while at work, my son called. I couldn't answer. I thought it was odd that he would call, but I had someone in my office and moved my phone to my drawer so I did not have to hear the buzzing continue. In a few moments, my office manager knocked on my door and asked to see me in the hall. I wanted to continue the intake that I had started with the person I was seeing. I looked at my office manager and said, "No, I will leave and someone else can do this." He nodded his head in agreement.

The office manager had given me a sticky note with a phone number to talk to the nurse at the hospital. She informed me my husband was about to be airlifted to a hospital out of the area. I headed to the hospital where they told me he was being medevacked four hours away. None of the hospitals that were closer could manage what needed to happen for him.

I had no idea as to the seriousness of the situation. I thought I could drive him there.

God did the miraculous in that situation. My husband ended up being operated on by one of the top aortic dissections specialists in the country. We were not spared the incident, but we were given the best care possible for my husband's recovery.

Disaster happens to all of us. This situation was not easy by any means. I look back now and think about how amazing all the pieces were put together. Even in the midst of it all, we were taken care of. Even in death, we are taken care of. God has already taken care of that in the provision of His Son. Know that no matter what, you are taken care of.

CHAPTER 27 BOOSTER #6

I ACCEPT THAT I AM IMPERFECT. HE IS MY PERFECTION.

That's a humbling thought. Isn't it?

I spent a good part of my life not being willing to accept my imperfection. No one ever told me He was my perfection. It's amazing what I did not learn in Sunday school. I learned I was a sinner, which seemed to be forever in my face. When that is all you focus on, it seems like it is the only path before you. I knew what not to do. I knew if I spent my whole life not doing that, I would be okay. But again, that was the focus. So, what hope is there in that?

I have a friend that teaches classes on how to ride a motorcycle. She uses the example that when you are riding and you see a tree, you don't focus on the tree. If the tree is your place of focus, that is where you will end up. It would really ruin your day too! The place of focus is the path around the tree with an awareness of the tree.

In this life we live, the path around the tree is God. When we focus on Him, we don't have to worry about the sin. We only need to be aware of the traps, however, they are not the focus. The important thing is to know where your focus is.

I also know part of the fear in my life came from focusing on the sin. I was so busy focusing on the sin and what not to do; I had no availability to the fun that I experience when I focus on Him. I was so afraid of sinning, of not living up to the plan, of missing God. With that much worry, how could I ever experience rest? I am reminded of Paul's Romans 7 discussion.

"For what I am doing, I do not understand. For what I will to do, that I do not practice; but what I hate, that I do" (Romans 7:15).

This was his way of telling the Roman Jews that the law does not work. He changes his focus from his failure to his Savior who has saved him from his own wretchedness. And with great proclamation, he announces something truly amazing in the first verse of the next chapter.

"There is therefore now no condemnation to those who are in Christ Jesus, who do not walk according to the flesh, but according to the Spirit. For the law of the Spirit of life in Christ Jesus has made me free from the law of sin and death" (Romans 8:1-2).

Paul declares there is a new law in town. It's the law of the Spirit of life. Now, there is your path around the tree.

With the reality that I'm no longer up for continual judgement or feeling like God is picking apart my every move, I am able to maneuver without hindrance into positive places. No longer do I have to live shackled to the law of my own focus and fear of my future, present or past sin. Sin is no longer a discussion I need to have with Him on an ongoing basis. It's me now focusing on Him. If I stumble, I repent. I ask for forgiveness wherever it is needed and dust myself off and move forward. It does not make sense for me to pay penance any longer. Jesus took care of that.

Penance may be a deep seated belief that you are not good enough. It may be about feeling like you don't deserve something because of wrong you have done. It may be choosing to not accept the grace of God and His forgiveness or your own because of something you did. My penance was deep guilt and immense self-blame. I think I blamed myself for everything. I felt that whatever happened, somehow, I was to blame. At the same time, I would temporarily shift the blame to someone else. I'm pretty sure I was not having any fun. I may have had moments that had laughter. I may have had moments of relief. I may have even felt positive emotions, at times. Internally, I was punishing myself for so many things that were old, dead and buried and I was the only one bringing them up. Like continual music playing in the background, my mind was busy punishing myself all the time. It may not have been the main theme, but it always set the stage for what was about to happen.

When I finished with graduate school, my husband and I went on a Caribbean cruise. I remember sitting on the deck in the evening. For the first time in my memory, my mind was quiet. It was a wonderful feeling. Every worry, concern and fear had gone on vacation too. I had even gotten up the nerve to go swimming with the sting rays on that trip. I don't know how that happened, but it did. It was also a foreshadowing of what would happen in my life seven years later when I went through deliverance. Once again, I would feel like I had a mind that was an empty canvas waiting to become a beautiful picture. Like the invitation was there to become a Monet or a Rembrandt instead of one that was filled with layers upon layers of paint that never made sense to the one looking at it.

CHAPTER 28 BOOSTER #7

I ACCEPT THAT I HAVE A PURPOSE IN THIS WORLD.

I wasn't born just to be born. Actually, my birth was kind of funny.

I was born on a Tuesday morning, which in itself is pretty unremarkable. However, you could never tell my mother that. I decided to be born breech. Not that breech births are uncommon, it was just butt first instead of the head first normal delivery. I find this amusing to this day, and I wonder what part of my makeup was committed to making such an entrance. I'm pretty sure my mother was not too happy, especially since I was her first born. I have wondered all my life what God was thinking as heaven must have needed a good laugh to orchestrate such a birth.

I believe heaven orchestrates to give us a purpose that is more wonderful than we will ever be able to imagine.

"That's why we have this Scripture text: No one's ever seen or heard anything like this, Never so much as imagined anything quite like it - What God has arranged for those who love him" (1 Corinthians 2:9, The Message).

To me that is one of the most fun verses in scripture. We cannot even imagine what God has for us. Even in your wildest, most over the top imagination, you would still miss it because at this point you don't have the ability to think that big. God is doing something so amazing, so wonderful, so beyond you that all you have to do is say yes to it and hop on board His love boat especially designed for you. I love this cruise, just get on board and say *yes*. And, don't just say yes, scream *yes*! Come into total agreement with Him, because arguing with Him is never fun and well, you might be wrong. I encourage you to make the adjustment in your brain. Remember the wonderful statement Jesus made, "Not my will, but your will." It's not always easy, but what an amazing payoff to always say yes to Him.

What is your purpose? Good question. There are lots of books out there on it. You could probably pick one up or read them all. The best possible thing to do is ask Him what your purpose is. You will probably find you are already in the process of discovery, otherwise you wouldn't be asking.

Sometimes we think it is easier to read a book about something with God than to go to Him. We are often intimidated by Him. I often think of the photographs of John Kennedy Jr. and Caroline playing in the White House's oval office while JFK worked. They were not intimidated. They were just children. How much more do we have access to our Heavenly Father who wants to give us the Kingdom?

I have all sorts of revelation around my purpose. I believe I am to bring the Kingdom wherever I go. I believe I am salt and light. I believe I am to write books and share this amazing thing called relationship which Jesus died for so the body of Christ could have it without the need to sweat for it. What I have learned from Father is that as long as I focus on Him, my purpose appears and the help for it happens too. If I ignore Him and do all sorts of things in my own mind and my own flesh, I get lost in thoughts of what I can and can't do and somewhere I get all jumbled up. When I look square into His eyes, I see everything so much clearly.

I accept that I am daily being made into the image of Jesus.

"God knew what He was doing from the very beginning. He decided from the outset to shape the lives of those who love Him along the same lines as the life of his Son. The Son stands first in the line of humanity He restored. We see the original and intended shape of our lives there in him" (Romans 8:29, The Message).

I know. Some cringe on this one. Yet, I think it is one of the most fun acknowledgements in my life. To accept this is to accept His kind hand in taking me beyond my own circumstances, way of thinking and limitations and leading me into the limitless life that has always been granted to me.

I have heard people talk about being made into the image of Jesus as if they are victims being tortured for the sake of the gospel. It's so sad. I love what Peter and John did after they were whipped for the gospel.

"The apostles went out of the High Council overjoyed because they had been given the honor of being dishonored on account of the Name" (Acts 5: 41, The Message).

Can you imagine anyone in our present day actually feeling grateful for being persecuted? I am very doubtful such a thing would happen in modern society. Most likely, we would tell everyone how horrible and difficult it was to evoke their sympathy. But imagine living in such joy that you look at your buddy and say, "Was that the most amazing honor or what?"

Dying to one's self is not difficult. It's admitting what I thought before was wrong, and experiencing living in the fun of the new me. The new me is able to love more. The new me is able to accept love more. The new me will mess other's up (in a good way) because they are expecting the old me to show up, not the new and improved, more like Jesus me. This me no one knows. And to be honest, I don't either because I haven't really taken me out for a test drive and seen how I will react to different situations where I reacted before. But, I'm going to try and I'm going to have fun. I've been upgraded. I've been given the keys to a newer, better me. When I look at me, I see more of Jesus and I'm grateful because He is beautiful. What an amazing life.

I accept that I am the salt of the earth.

"You are the salt of the earth. But if the salt loses its saltiness, how can it be made salty again? It is no longer good for anything, except to be thrown out and trampled underfoot" (Matthew 5:13).

Did you taste that? It was flat, yucky, without any depth. That's a swift idea of how I felt the one and only time I tasted poi, which tastes like slightly apple flavored wall paper paste. Although, I doubt salt would have improved it, but you get the idea. Several foods are tasteless without salt.

I feel that way about potatoes and most meats. To me, they are boring without salt. Some people don't care for salt, while others should not have it for medical reasons. I'm not one of them. I even like grinding my own pink Himalayan salt. Doing so releases its minerals on my food increasing the nutritional value of my meal.

I like the idea of designer salts. I remember as a kid all we had was the girl under the umbrella on the blue box. Salt was about making sure you got your iodine so you didn't have thyroid problems. Then they introduced sea salt because it was supposed to be better and then the pink salt came along. I wonder if there aren't different kinds of us out there in the kingdom being different kinds of salt. Whatever kind of salt we are, what is important is that we are adding flavor, because without us, the world is flat.

You see, our very presence brings flavor, the unexpected flavor of a different life. When we are present, hope is also present. When we—the flavor of the world—are absent, people don't know there is a promise of freedom from the enemy and from themselves. They don't know there is more to this life than working, entertainment and death. We are the ones who exhibit that through our own lives and beliefs, through our own flavor in any given situation.

You see, being salt isn't about doing anything or having to make something happen. It's just about being salt. There is really nothing else we can be but amazing children—sons and daughters that we have always been, being changed from glory to glory and watching the world look at us in amazement because of His incredible hand in our life. It's from here, being ourselves, having fun, basking in His great love and accepting that His love is so much more than we yet know, that we are able to be okay and allow people to come up to us and see what a life of flavor looks like. We may even have to be okay with allowing people to taste us.

"Oh, taste and see that the Lord is good; Blessed is the man who trusts in Him" (Psalm 34: 8, NKJV).

If He tastes good, aren't you going to? Don't you have the same Spirit in you? People need to see what your life is made of. They need (yes, need, like water and air) to see this Spirit in you that raised Christ from the dead, because it is amazing. Their desire to leave bland food alone will cause them to inquire about what kind of salt you are. You'll be able to introduce others to the salt even as you were initially introduced to a life of amazing flavor. What a fun life you live.

PART V THE THIEVES AND BEYOND

Chapter 29 Navigating Through

This section is committed to realizations about our life that are important to have to complete the fun cycle. As we realize these things about ourselves, we are able to navigate past them quickly and move into a new frame of mind— a place to talk to God about where you are and where you want to go. The focus is discussion with Him that will bring you into deeper relationship. This is always the best option.

The *fun busters* are also part of this section. I am sure there will not be any surprises, just reminders. Where you find yourself desiring freedom from the busters, talk to Him. He will direct your path. Be patient with yourself as you embrace a greater level of His love for you.

I realize that the only person stopping me from having fun is me.

"If you could kick the person in the pants responsible for most of your trouble, you wouldn't sit for a month." Theodore Roosevelt

What a responsible thing to realize, especially when I could blame shift. I could blame my husband, my kids, the pastor, the church, the dog, my parents, the government, my boss, my job, the economy, etc. I bet you could even add a few more.

How is it we so easily blame someone else for what we have the power to change? What makes us believe that our circumstances have a right to determine our mind set? Many have been in difficult situations, yet they have learned to rejoice. Martyrs before us have been joyous in the worst of circumstances and we complain when our burger does not arrive quick enough. How did we lose our joy over "first world problems"?

It's amazing how many there are of them. We complain about the way they pressed our laundry when we took our clothes to the cleaners. The car in front of us stalled on the road and we had to go around them. They aren't driving fast enough, even though we left late. We don't understand why there is a line at the drive up window. We demand a personal shopper to cater to us at the department store.

When we were in Thailand, we spent some time in places that were not anywhere close to health department standards. We used disgusting toilets that had no resemblance to western culture toilets. We shared pictures of our experience with many of our friends. I was amazed at how many said they would not use that. I was so grateful there was one available.

We have come to a place of entitlement. We want to blame everyone and everything else for our thoughts and our behavior. "I'm yelling because you made me mad!" "I only reacted that way because you did that."

I was once told, there is no time like the present. Now is the time to become aware of what we are really doing. Think about this, living life on autopilot is no fun. We tend to do what is the most pressing or whatever is the most demanding at the time. Perhaps shut down has set in and life is sitting in front of the TV. Maybe, it's a life driven by an unknown force that places us in that chair, that argument, or that store shopping when there is so much more to life than a mindless way of living. What if our lives became intentional, conscious moments strung together in time instead of the regular ongoing, not thinking, just doing kind of life where our mind plays the same old worry song over and over?

What does the conscious life look like? It looks like living in the moment and welcoming the moment you are in, capturing where you are and what you are doing and the presence of God within it. It is a place of the most amazing worship and rest. It's a place of embracing yourself and being embraced in the most marvelous way possible. It is full minutes turning into full days of a life that is abundant. It's not wishing that we were. It's grasping that we are. We are loved. We are held. We are taken care of. It's not about anything other than that moment of time and yet even in that moment of time, we can embrace what we are feeling. In that rest and consciousness, our future can be planned from a place of delight.

Knowing that I am responsible for my life does not make me bad if I am not where I wish I was by now. It means I have the ability to reach out to the One who has a better path for me. I can find myself in deeper relationship with Him and taking myself into that relationship, I will find myself in a better place. The fun part is the adventure in all of this. If we are not careful, we will forget that life is an adventure. Then, we will find ourselves without rest. And there, once again we move into that relationship with God that is filled with dry bones and old law.

I realize I don't know everything.

""For My thoughts are not your thoughts, Nor are your ways My ways," says the Lord" (Isaiah 55:8, NKJV).

I like this scripture. Though, I forget it often. It plays into my need to be perfectionistic. I also use to never like being wrong. That really got me down. I use to think I had to be right all the time. Someone who has to be right all the time is very difficult to be married to, to be friends with and to love. A person that has to be right all the time doesn't really allow others to exist within their sphere. They only allow what is a reflection of what they believe is their own selves within the relationship. There is this really fun part about God that I love. He is right all the time. Yet, He is never threatened by our challenging Him or asking Him about His decisions. He is so confident in Himself, He can live with our need to ask questions within our limited knowledge. Oh, to have a secure God that we know so we also can be secure.

It took a while for me to realize I didn't know everything. Sure, I knew I did not know everything. However, in my life there was no practice of it. I gave everyone my opinion. I even told strangers what I thought whether they asked me or not. I was arrogant and confident that I knew what was best for everyone. Then the Lord in His great kindness began to show me how little I knew and how much He knew.

You don't learn how little you know overnight. It may take years to really understand. Before I really began to understand this, I had to ask for something called humility, which was painful. It's like God took the top of my skull off and allowed me to look into my brain and realize there was some really icky stuff in there. I didn't want to touch it. I really didn't want someone else to touch it, but I went ahead and let Him touch all that stuff. I knew without His touch I would stay the same, and somehow, deep down inside I knew I was miserable.

The greatest deception of my life has been believing that I was perfectly good when I was, in fact, miserable, unhappy and joyless. No one could have ever told me I was unhappy. I had spent a lot of time telling myself I was happy because that was what a Christian did. I put on a happy face. What I did not reckon with while I was busy putting on that face was how concerned I was that somehow someone somewhere would think Jesus was not all He was cracked up to be. I believed I was the one person in the world that had to hold it all together for the sake of God. After all, if we as Christians didn't know everything and weren't a happy representative of the Gospel, who would believe? And if no one else believed, then I would have failed God and I did not want to do that. I desperately needed His approval.

At the time, I did not know I already had His approval. I spent so much time grabbing and grasping, I missed this verse that I knew so well.

"To the praise of the glory of His grace, by which He made us accepted in the Beloved" (Ephesians 1:6, NKJV).

Did you see that? I (and you, of course) am accepted by what He did. For the longest time, I have walked around meditating on it, told others about it, yet nothing about it in my life appeared to know that truth.

At one point in my life, I began to take a look at my relationships. I found that being right from my own insecure place was not enriching other people or me. I began to watch what I was saying and how I was addressing these relationships. What I discovered was amazing.

One day, I realized it was actually freeing to not have to know everything. It was fun to learn new things. I learned to say, "Oh, I didn't know that." Or, "You're right." These are sentences I previously would never have said. It was difficult to guide the words over my tongue and out of my mouth at first. Eventually, they became a smile on my face and I began to see them as a fun part of life. Admitting I was wrong in my life allowed me to admit I was also wrong about some of the ways I saw God. Being wrong became a wonderful thing.

There is something about losing the need to be right and accepting His grace that goes hand and hand. I no longer needed to know everything about what was going on in our relationship. While He was working to help me accept me, He was all about letting me know He loves me. There has been such freedom in His love, so much more than there ever was in being right. The more I accept that I don't have to be right, the more I accept His awesome plan for me. I have also learned in my other relationships that the desire to love others trumps the need to be right. That way, everyone wins.

For those who are wondering, let me set the record straight. There is no compromise on some things. I don't compromise on the truth of the Bible or the truth of the God of the Bible. It is truth. It's not about me being right. It's about Him being God. I don't have to make that happen and I don't have to defend it because it defends itself. I don't get into arguments with argumentative people, but I will certainly sit down and have a glass of water with anyone who is openly seeking. I'm not interested in doing Holy Spirit's job anymore. I used to think I needed to. That too went away with my need to be right. What remains, I hope, is salt, light and curiosity.

Curiosity is a remarkable way to look at God's world. Now, I can ask necessary questions that inspire wonder. I can look for more understanding, no longer presuming *I know*. This life is about looking to Him and seeing what He wants to show me. I can be curious and adventurous as I continue to look into the King of the Universe and desire Him to show me more.

CHAPTER 30 FUN BUSTERS

There are things that will hinder fun. I have listed six below. However, in no way is this list exhaustive. Maybe you have more and will notice what they are as you journey on your adventure towards fun. As you head toward this undertaking, it's important to remember that fun is vital to your vibrant relationship with God. Fun makes a difference in how we see our lives. It breaks up the hold religious ways have on us.

Shame

Shame is the sense that something is horribly wrong with me and whatever I get I deserve. It's the idea that whatever is wrong with this picture, I must be it. It's the mindset that I am unlovable. I am not able. I am so bad I could never do anything. I am so unworthy I could never amount to anything.

Shame is degrading. When we give way to it, we find ourselves crushed and unable to move. It tends to wrap itself around us and strangle us like a big old python. Shame is a nasty critter. How do I know? I used to be a major carrier.

The problem with shame is it will stop everything in your life. It takes away your confidence and convinces you that nothing you do will ever be good enough. It can be pervasive for some people, keeping them completely blinded to their gifts and talents because somehow they believe they are not enough and they will never be enough.

Shame is also contagious. You can shame other people easily and people will take it on. When you experience shame, it feels rotten to the bones and dries them out. Often people are shamed in their religious beliefs. It goes something like, "I thought you were a good Christian." Or, "you should really do more because you obviously don't hear from God." People will use shame to motivate and control us into what they think we should do. This is a deadly combo when we are already attached to the harmful effects of shame.

My husband and I were sure we had heard God clearly when we put our house on the market and prepared to move to Florida from Washington State. The church we were in, at the time, was not so sure. We heard from one man that his sister had missed it in putting her house on the market and the implication was we had missed it as well and needed to stay where we were. Well, I knew what I had heard and I was not going to let him shame me because God had not acted as quickly as I would have liked Him to. I ignored the comment and continued to believe for what I had heard. When the house did sell, it could not have been a better time. It came within forty-eight hours after a word from the pulpit told the congregation our move was from God. It was as if you could hear the congregation exhale. The house sold, freeing us to go where we were being called to go.

I have learned that shame is not necessary in the body of Christ. Shame is a way of trying to control others. I realize the person mentioned previously really wanted us to stay. However, shame is often about control. The reality of control among Christians is all too familiar. When we use shame to control others or try to keep ourselves in check, we will find we are out of the fun zone and living in a heavy laden cage.

What is the heavy laden cage? The place Jesus wants to take us from.

"Come to me all you who are weary and heavy laden and I will give you rest. Take this yoke upon me and learn from me for I am humble and lowly of heart, and you will find rest for your souls" (Matthew 11:28-29, NKJV).

The heavy laden cage is a prison imposed by yourself and others filled with *you should* and *do this* and *do that*, which is not relationship with God. It is religion meant to control and the essence of why Jesus was always so angry at the Pharisees.

The body of Christ would be better off without shame. All of us would find an amazing sense of freedom without shame. A lot of us have spent so much time with shame, we think it is a way of life. Jesus bore our shame on the cross, so we no longer have to let it control our lives.

Jesus has given us hope in moving past shame.

"Therefore, it is also contained in the Scripture, "Behold, I lay in Zion A chief cornerstone, elect, precious, And He who believes on Him will by no means be put to shame"" (I Peter 2:6).

My concern is that most people don't recognize their shame programming. Asking Holy Spirt to guide you will begin the healing process so you are able to live a wonderfully vulnerable life. This process will free you to no longer have to hide behind what you do out of fear of being found lacking in the judgement of others. You don't have to be afraid, neither do you have to conceal your amazing self from the world.

CHAPTER 31 UNFORGIVENESS

"Unforgiveness is like drinking poison yourself and waiting for the other person to die."

- Marianne Williamson

Unforgiveness is a wet blanket. It rots the human spirit. Holding a grudge does not work for anyone. For some reason we can easily forgive others, or at least we say that, but forgiving ourselves is another story.

For a good portion of my life, I walked in unforgiveness towards myself. I was caught up in the myth that if I forgave myself it would be too permissive and I would be letting myself off the hook way too easily. I also thought if I let myself off the hook, somehow I would be opening a door to doing the very thing I was mad at myself for. I was locked in chains, feeling that I was responsible to keep me on task, making sure I did not do those things I was so afraid I would do.

I allowed bitterness to grapple my soul on a continuous basis. I participated in other behaviors to deal with the pain, as opposed to actually forgiving myself and allowing myself to experience the full benefit of the Love of God being poured out for me.

Shame and unforgiveness danced together to wrap me up. Shame would tell me how bad I was, then unforgiveness would say I could not forgive myself because I might do it again. The two were close friends of mine and I listened to them for a very long time. I did not even realize what was going on until the Lord Himself interrupted me and decided His love for me was greater than my own ability to undo what He was trying to do in my life.

A normal day, like any other, the Lord decided to show up and make it an extraordinary day. I heard Him say, "You wear shame like a corset." I saw scissors come down from heaven and remove what the enemy wanted me to be tied up in. The one thing I knew from watching movies was that a corset does not allow you room to breathe.

It was not as easy as that one moment. But, that was the beginning. He has stepped in with His kindness over the years and has shown me the blind spots involved in shame and the undoing of the demonic training. It has taken years. We still work on it. I am grateful for His persistence. He wants me free. He wants me to have fun. That day He came after my shame was an incredible moment. We were able to address the unforgiveness as well. Our determination in this matter has been joyous.

CHAPTER 32 SIN

Sin seems obsolete in a politically correct world. In my field, most refer to sin as poor choices. I'm with the great philosopher, Steve Taylor when he asked, "Whatever happened to sin?" I think this is an appropriate question in our present culture. There are so many ways to react to sin, I often see why our culture tried to make it obsolete. Perhaps there is another way to look at it.

When I sin, or work out of a place that separates me from God, I do myself a great injustice which affects the entire body of Christ. Sin is not an isolated incident. Its effects go beyond you. To say it doesn't affect anyone else is not true.

When I damage my relationship with God, I am not offering my best self in the moment. When I cut any part of my relationship off with God, even in the smallest measure, I am affected and I affect others around me because I carry either guilt, a shutdown self or some distraction that places me in a position to not bring my best self to the table. Any way you look at it, we all lose out. When I harm my relationship with my Creator, all my relationships are harmed.

Sin is also viral. When someone else sins and we give them the ability to influence us, we choose to let down our guard and ignore what Holy Spirit speaks to us. When we make the chasm in our relationship with God, we are left with shame and the feeling of separation that hurts us and those around us.

If I sin, I have learned I am to repent quickly. I ask for forgiveness and the strength and fortification within my relationship with Him to never repeat my sinful behavior again. If I have hurt someone, I must attempt to heal our relationship. If the relationship cannot be healed, for some horrendous reason, I talk with God and enjoy His presence as I mourn, knowing He has not left me. This is a life changing process, which makes it fun. It may not always seem fun when I'm walking through it, especially if I've hurt someone important to me.

CHAPTER 33 FEAR

Fear is a nasty beast. Isn't it? The enemy is rotten in how he plays this hand. When we are walking in fear, it is nearly impossible to have fun. Usually fear is so blinding that fun is illusive. Fear is a thief. There is no peace when fear is around.

Fear is unbearable. How many destinies have been stolen from fear? How many people had opportunities to do amazing adventures but were side swiped by fear? Have you? I know I have.

When Jesus said the thief comes to steal, kill and destroy, I am sure the first thing on his list was fear. This is the most insidious tool of the enemy. The essence of fear is to disarm you to a place where you cannot do something. If you are able to do what you are supposed to do in that moment, you feel the rush and excitement of that moment. It's exhilarating to do what the moment requires. If you make excuses because of fear, you are robbing yourself. Fear steals what is rightly yours. All too often or too easily, we agree with it. It steals your fruit, your life, and your ability to feel safe. Fear is a scoundrel that has to be reckoned with.

Many times in my life, I have taken on my own fear. Now, I know people don't talk about these things as it makes them vulnerable. But then, that is fear that keeps us from it. The best way I know to deal with fear is to walk through it and not let it continue in my life.

In the early stages of my career as a Marriage and Family therapist, I would take my cases to what we call supervision. In order to become a licensed professional, so many hours of supervision are required. For an hour or two every couple of weeks, I would choose to present at least one case. The decision as to which one was always mine. At some point, I realized I could either choose the case I was doing the best on, which would make me look good, or I could choose the one I was most challenged by, which would help me grow as a therapist.

At the time, I operated from a high level of shame. It was so much easier to talk about what I was doing right and really difficult to consider the fact that I needed help. I so wanted to look good all the time, even at my client's expense. Holy Spirit being so kind to me reminded me that if I walked in fear, fear was all I would ever walk in. So, with all the courage I could muster I presented my most challenging cases affording me the opportunity to be blessed in learning from some of the most seasoned and brilliant minds in this business I have ever known. Going beyond my fear produced fruit in my life at that time and still does.

Becoming aware of fear is a whole different story altogether. Most people no longer recognize their fear. They easily justify it to themselves. I have people in my life that talk about being afraid on a regular basis. I have a young friend that does not want to go abroad for vacation because she is worried about not getting reception on her phone. I believe if we had not mentioned it to her, she would have never realized how fear was shaping her decisions. She is now hoping to take a cruise for her first wedding anniversary.

What kind of fears people have is not the important question. The important question is what kind of fears do you have? When you find your fears, you can overcome them. I used to be afraid of public speaking. I realized the problem wasn't fear of speaking to a crowd. I feared what people would think of me. When I got to a place where God turned me upside down and talked to me about not fearing man, all that changed. He showed me I could not love people if I feared them at that level and I would never be able to minister to them. In our conversations, He illuminated that public speaking was the same as one on one, a point of teaching heart to heart. If I paid attention to that, He would give me the words and I would learn to love people and not fear them in this way. He is so smart, that I am in such a need of him. I would never have come up with these revelations on my own.

Anxiety is fear exemplified. Anxiety can be continuous worry, like bad music playing in the background. People have a foreboding sense that something may go wrong or has already gone wrong. People who live in anxiety run to whatever they can in that moment to divert their attention from the fears that continually haunt them. Anxiety is not reasonable. It is unable to coexist with the deep fun we are talking about. Anxiety must be dealt with through addressing the roots of fear. You may also desire deliverance. Paul gives us a great answer for anxiety and worry:

"Don't fret or worry. Instead of worrying, pray. Let petitions and praises shape your worries into prayers, letting God know your concerns. Before you know it, a sense of God's wholeness, everything coming together for good, will come and settle you down. It's wonderful what happens when Christ displaces worry at the center of your life" (Philippians 4: 6-7, The Message).

So, again, what are you anxious about? What are you afraid of? Are you afraid of what people will think of you? Most of us are.

In 2001, I went through something called Prophetic Deliverance, which began the most amazing freedom I have ever known. I am very grateful Father brought me to it. The actual deliverance was easy. It was the walking it out afterwards that took a greater level of courage. After that event, the Lord set me aside in life. I spent time with my journal in a back room in my house for multiple hours every day. What I learned at that time was a remarkable biblical principle that Paul taught:

"Casting down arguments and every high thing that exalts itself against the knowledge of God, bringing every thought into captivity to the obedience of Christ" (2 Corinthians 10:5).

Together, Father and I took on every fear I could possibly have for nearly two years. We would talk about all my fears. It was amazing. I am sure someone reading this will say, "That sounds exhausting!" On the contrary, it was exhilarating because with the disarming of each fear came freedom. It was fun, amazing fun, because at the end of each time I walked away with less fear and more of a sense of trusting Him in a greater way. Fear erodes trust. It really does. Without trust, faith is nearly impossible. Are you afraid of losing control? Are you afraid of the future, the past or this very moment? What I learned from losing my fears was that I could move towards being the fully alive, fully free person I was always called to be.

This has brought tremendous change in my life. Telling you I love to travel would be an understatement. In the days where fear ruled my life, I used to bring everything. Those were the years when you could take two large suitcases that weighed seventy pounds each across country. I was going on a cruise with five other couples and wanted to bring my own bottled water. I loaded a large suitcase full. My husband was not happy that I had packed so many bags as he had to carry them. When we reached the terminal to check our luggage, the airline agent told me the suitcase was too heavy. I was so afraid I wouldn't have something I made my husband and myself miserable in the process.

Now, I travel with one suitcase that is less than fifty pounds for the both of us. If necessary, I bring a small carryon and maybe one that looks like a large purse so I can carry snacks for a long ride under the seat in front of me. I only bring that much when we go on long vacations so I can bring back souvenirs. I realized not taking four large suitcases and four carry-ons have become freedom. I take what I need and leave space for getting things to give to those I love. The rest is unnecessary. The fun part is if I forget something I go looking for it, which can be hysterical when we don't speak the same language. Once, I went looking for dental floss in a drug store in a Paris suburb. It was a silly moment trying to describe dental floss even with a French American dictionary. Eventually, we did get the floss. The memory still brings all types of pictures to my mind. I can only smile at the amusement God has afforded me.

Fighting my way through my own fear has been significant. Part of finding my way through fear is to think about what I think and what I feel. This process taught me to no longer be afraid of what I think or what I feel. Just because I feel or think something does not make me bad. It means I may need to pay attention and filter my thoughts and my feelings. I did learn that with each fear comes a lie. When each lie is revealed and truth is exposed, the chains fall off and relief comes. What I have learned with time is that I was experiencing the perfect love from God that John speaks of.

"There is no fear in love; but perfect love casts out fear, because fear involves torment. But He who fears has not been made perfect in love. We love Him because He first loved us" (1 John 4:18-19, NKJV).

I like it when things are easy. What about your relationship with Father can shift so you can accept His perfect love that will help you trust Him? What in your feelings of fear are you willing to trade for His perfect love? What do you think would happen if you asked for His perfect love? Maybe you would get what you have desired, peace from those fears that hold you back. Maybe then you could go and do what you have always wanted to do but never had the courage for. Talk to Him about His perfect love and wait and see what He does. He absolutely knows what He is doing.

One last thing to address is the fear of the Lord. This is a different fear. The fear of the Lord is the beginning of wisdom. When we desire the fear of the Lord, everything shifts. The fear of the Lord is not a being scared of, it's a being in awe of. When we are in awe, we are consumed by a loving God who is trustworthy. The fear of the Lord does not torment us as the fears of this world do. The fear of the Lord comforts and secures us.

CHAPTER 34 PERFECTIONISM

"Grace is the face that love wears when it meets imperfection."

— Joseph R. Cooke

I introduce my opposition to perfectionism not as an excuse to do a poor job on anything. That is not the purpose of this. It's to loose the shackles we find ourselves in because of our own doing. We find our way into the pain of perfectionism through a belief system that subscribes to our inability to feel we measure up to Christ's sacrifice for us. Few of us actually exchange our own perfectionistic tendencies for the reality of His grace in our lives.

Perfectionism is painful. It's the inability to accept imperfection or the belief that we must always do more to be good enough, to qualify, to be loved. It's very demanding on the person and those around them. It makes room for ongoing rejection of people and the person. It closes doors and leaves misery behind it. The perfectionist is not about doing a job well, but having a standard so high no one can live up to it, not even themselves. The perfectionist is usually hardest on themselves.

The perfectionist's thoughts often play along the lines of, "it has to look like this (insert requirements here) before I can accept it." The perfectionist demands that what has played out in their mind is to be their reality. Perfectionists do not know how to live within a reasonable place where grace is always at play and enjoy a relationship with God where they no longer give into feelings of separation.

One example of perfectionistic tendencies is the person that goes from marriage to marriage and blames all the marriage failure on the former husbands. Maybe, it's the woman who got divorced because her spouse didn't live up to her expectations. Instead of building acceptance within the relationship, she threw him overboard because her expectations for marriage didn't include him as a person. Or, it could be the man or woman who never gets married because they are not willing to risk themselves to a less than perfect mate. Another example might be the person who does not apply for the job in a tight job market because it isn't what they want or perhaps, they think they don't quite have all the skills it will take to do the job right.

I used to hold myself and others up to a high standard. I was not happy and it mostly happened because I did not feel like I was good enough. I was pretty sure I did not measure up anywhere. That is how we see things isn't it? I was very unforgiving, especially towards myself. I did not allow forgiveness towards myself even though Jesus had long forgiven me. I even continued to bring up my imperfections to Him so that we were both on the same page. Isn't that sad?

Eventually, He nearly moved heaven and earth to teach me about a word called grace. Even though I had always known the word grace as having been saved by grace, I did not know the impact grace could have on my life.

Grace gave me the ability to forgive myself. It gave me the ability to accept that I needed a savior. It gave me the gift to find my way to the bridge to love. I believe grace fought for me when I could not fight for myself because I was so committed to my focus on my imperfections instead of His great love. But grace does that. It comes after you and demands you look it square on until all you see is the acceptance of Jesus's smile staring you straight on. With that, grace steps in and begins to heal the heart from your own harsh and unmerciful ways. That is what He did to me anyway.

Without His grace stepping up to the plate, I would still be lost in my own need for perfection and demanding the same from everyone else. I realize now that my thinking was the result of my culture as it runs along the lines of needing things to be perfect. After all, you would not watch a cooking show if they burnt the food. When we look in a magazine, we see perfect models. We prefer the young and the beautiful, or so I gather from looking at the advertisements. We don't think about the airbrush that helps them all look so good. Perfect sells. The imperfect people don't sell unless we enjoy watching crazy families on TV. Somehow seeing others imperfections makes us feel better about ourselves. It adds comfort, giving us the idea that maybe we are not so imperfect after all. We could show them how to do it right because, of course, we know how to do that.

I spent a good chunk of my thirties in therapy. I paid someone who helped me break away from my need to stand in continual judgement of my imperfections and it was money well spent. I called my harsh internal verdicts "being hard on myself." I was relentless and shame clouded my every thought somewhere in the background of my mind. It was not easy living in shame and the demands I put on myself. I did not know how difficult it had been until the shift away from that thinking took place. I was continually down on myself for the littlest things. My weight wasn't right. My grades in school weren't good enough. As a parent, I did not reach my invisible mark. Part of this microscopic gaze included not responding to people in the right way. I felt as though I was always failing. One day, I came to the most brilliant conclusion. It was so simple, yet it changed everything, I really needed a savior. I didn't need one just a little bit, I needed one a lot. I needed one that could save me from me, from my need to be perfect. I needed one to save me from my need to impress Him and earn His love. I needed Him to be what I could not be, which was perfect. I really needed a savior.

In the years since, I have shifted much of what I believe about perfection. Now, I can say that I love imperfection. One of the things I do through work is encourage others to embrace their imperfection. I find teaching people to rest in love is a great way to address perfectionism. When people know they are loved, really loved, it often fills the vacuum and dislodges perfectionism over time. They will find that love is such a better option over picking one's self apart.

For a season, I was involved in a weekly mentoring call with a group of young women. It was a delightful time. Every week, we went to unplanned places in our conversation. I often wish I would have written them down afterwards because they were so enjoyable and book worthy.

There was one time when someone on the call said, "I am perfect and I never will be." This was such a thrilling revelation. It allowed acceptance to enter the call. There was so much release that went on. You see, we can be more than one thing at a time. We can be perfectly accepted by God in Christ who is perfect, and we can be imperfect and accept ourselves in our imperfections. It's really a wonderful place to rest and quit having to strive for the impossible. Besides, Jesus already did the impossible. I am sure that was enough.

Chapter 35 Living the Life of the Victim

Eeyore is a great character in Winnie the Pooh but not in real life. I meet Eeyore's all the time and they are difficult to be around. They suck the life out of the room. And, to be honest, they often love their misery. I have known a few Eeyore's and they seldom have the charm of their name sake, who at moment's notice turns things into a positive spin. In my experience, humans who fit this type seldom do. Extreme Eeyore personalities attempt to convince others their life is full of doom and gloom and they need you to be a part of their perilous tornado.

It's then, when you see them coming that you want to hide. The real truth is we all have a bit of Eeyore in us that we must be attentive to or we will find people running from us as well.

I used to live the victim. I wanted people to feel sorry for me. It was easier to live off of people's pity than their encouragement. I had no idea it was even possible to live off encouragement and positive feedback. I did not know I could think differently and make different choices about the way I thought. I thought that making up excuses for where I was not in life was a way to live. I was not even aware taking responsibility for my life was important. I didn't know I had choices. I only thought I had fate pulling me through life like I was being pulled through a knothole. I created my own disaster wherever I went. After all, that is what I did.

There was a time in my life where Holy Spirit insisted I move into the personal growth arena. We were at a conference and a special speaker presented what his company did and how they trained people to think differently about life. I am convinced Holy Spirit picked me up by my collar and took me to the place where the speaker was and signed me up. To be quite honest, He yelled in my ear, "You need this." Everything would change as a result of that day. Everything!

It would introduce me to people who no longer made excuses for what they did. They made choices that propelled them forward. Choices that were good, not just filled with lazy river lives that floated but lives that moved from one vantage point to another vantage point. These people were making choices that led them into a life lived with purpose, not happenstance. It was uncomfortable to have so many people around me that were interested in my success. I had not known that in my life, or at least had not been able to grab it from those that understood it. It was very unnerving at first. I remember thinking at times I wanted to jump out the window like the lion in the *Wizard of Oz* when he faced the wizard for the first time. I was continually in that feeling for a while. I learned to enjoy the uncomfortableness of it. I believe I had filled my life with so many contrary perceptions of myself that actually believing I could do something amazing seemed too beyond me and too beyond God's dreams for me. Eventually, I would have to address my own victim thinking.

How did I address my own victim thinking? At first, I changed my words. Sounds simple, right? Not so much. These were words that were well imbedded into my vocabulary. It was not all that easy.

One day, I was on a call with a friend. He said to me, "You can no longer say *but*, *should*, *try*, or *need*. If you say any of those words, you owe me five dollars each time you do and you will put the money aside and give it to charity." I said, "Okay," and swallowed heavily. I did not realize how much my language was part of my problem. I did not want to pay for my language, so I had to concentrate on what I was saying, which was a real ordeal for me at the time (remember, I was not getting this fun thing at this point). I learned when I said *but* that it was negating everything that went before it. I had often heard in my life, "I love you, but. . ." which to me always meant the person who said it really didn't love me.

Should was an interesting word to tackle in my vocabulary as well. It has a purpose all on its own. Its purpose was to shame me. I should have done this. I should have done that . . . You can also get the same results with *could* or *would*. What I found is that *I will do this* is a much stronger statement than I should have done this. *I will* is forward moving and puts me in the direction I am looking for.

After changing my vocabulary and determining that being a victim was not something I wanted to be, I found myself empowered. God encouraged me to walk alongside Him, no longer saying I should but saying, "I am accepting this walk with I AM." Moving past the excuses into the place of forward motion moved me out of my own lackluster life into a journey that presented a new world where I was experiencing empowerment in my walk with God I had not experienced before, and I really liked it.

Chapter 36 Obvious Ways to Have Fun with God

Games with God

I have plenty of friends that travel in the prophetic and experience different symbols from God as an affirmation of where they are going in their life. I have a friend who sees different numbers he is supposed to pay attention to on receipts, license plates and buses. Things show up for him and he knows it has some relevance in his life. For him, it's like a puzzle. He and God are always on a hunt to find the next confirming piece so they can chuckle together.

God has been playing a game with me as of late. I've been finding all these dimes. I found one on the floor at the store. I have found them in the wash machine, on the sidewalk. Wherever I go, I find these dimes. I have found lots of pennies in my life. In fact, I find pennies all the time and I always pick them up. But dimes are like ten times more than I am used to and I just laugh. I still have not figured out exactly what it means. I think it means my journey is about to change, so I'm waiting to see how that happens. Ultimately, it means I get to rest and cooperate with Him as I see Him unfold what I have yet to imagine.

"It is the glory of God to conceal a matter, But the glory of kings is to search out a matter" (Proverbs 25: 2).

I think this is what God loves to do with us. He's like a Father that hides a present, a treasure waiting for us to find it so we can enjoy it together. I have found this to be true in so many ways that I am amazed at how it looks.

I get dreams and visions on all sorts of things. He gives them to me as amazing gifts, each one beckoning me to look at these remarkable puzzles He and I are putting together. He is always throwing out things He wants to show me so I desire a deeper place in him, fueling my desire to want to know more of Him. It's in all these things I find a greater level of His faithfulness and enjoy His company. He doesn't throw all this out to frustrate me and keep me hopeless. Not at all. Everything is an invitation to a deeper walk with Him. I am a king who will search out the matters He brings my way. I often feel like a child. I squeal with delight when we find our way into the answer He has for me. Oh, this is fun.

There was a season where God talked to me through nature. He wanted to show me the wonders of it. He told me to go into my backyard one day when we lived in Florida. I was delighted when I went back there and found a turtle laying her eggs. All I could think about was the wonder that He was showing me. If I had brushed off His invitation, I would have missed something amazing. Not long after that, we visited family in Washington State. A hummingbird came within eighteen inches of my face and looked at me as if I was the interesting one. I was in awe again of these sweet things He showed me. I wondered when He would show me the next thing. The expectation was part of the fun of it all.

Nature

"For you shall go out with joy, And be led out with peace; The mountains and the hills Shall break forth into singing before you, And all the trees of the field shall clap their hands" (Isaiah 55:12, NKJV).

I love nature. It's amazing to me. While I have shared a couple of stories about nature, there is so much more.

Brother Lawrence found nature the place he originally grabbed God. There, he would get lost in the splendor of it all.

I find the creation and the Creator tied together without any chasm. When I see a red headed woodpecker, I stand in awe and wonder of creation and how He has put it all together. When I see a pregnant woman or a baby, I am reminded of His amazing ability to create what I could not begin to do. When experiencing a sunny day, I grab it. I breathe it in and rejoice in the One who made it. There is so much to Him and how He has created this world.

I love storms. When I see one on the way, something inside of me yells, *nice*. Not that I always find them convenient, because sometimes I won't venture out in them. I don't prefer to shop wet. Yet, the noise, the wind, the lightning all display His splendor. How can the theatrics not be loved? It's like He reminds us of who He is and how powerful He is. There is safety in that. Embracing the wonder of creation is fun.

Butterflies are a wonder to me. God often shows me His delight through butterflies, usually allowing me to see them in multitude. Bugs crack me up. Here in Georgia, they can be huge. I'm not crazy about snakes, but I learned they can be full of color when we lived in Florida. I'm not crazy about non domesticated rats or mice. However, I don't have to like everything. I can still be amazed.

Expectation

You see, I expect God to be fun. Expectation is important in our relationship with Him. It dictates a lot. If we do not expect, what can we hope for? We are encouraged to expect if you look at what is said in the Bible. The guy in the temple looked at Peter and John expecting something for his begging. Blind Bartimaeus expected Jesus to answer his yelling. The father expected Jesus to cast the demon out of his son. Expectation is important and a key in the kingdom. I expect Father to be fun. It's when we don't expect that we often get a result we don't plan for.

Abraham did not expect Sarah to get pregnant, so he went into the servant girl and she gave birth to Ishmael. That pretty much made his family life a mess for a long time.

Ahab didn't expect to lose in battle and listened to the prophets that he was told were lying. It cost him his life.

The enemy did not expect Jesus to rise again. That cost him much more than he ever thought was possible.

I have learned that expecting is much more fun than living without hope. The two go hand in hand, and can be applied to this idea of living an exciting life with God. Your life was never meant to be dull. It was never meant to be without hope. It was never meant to be a bunch of rules. Your life was meant for you to walk hand and hand with your Creator in the most amazing intimacy you have ever known. Life is to be known, to know that you are known and to delight in being known because you no longer have to prove anything.

A walk in a garden; that is all life was ever meant to be. A walk. It was to be filled with laughter, smiles, revelation, understanding, growth, delight and more laughter. I have often wondered if we have lost so much of that. Maybe we lost some of it for a season, but I think the invitation is here to get it back. Jesus died to restore us to this place of intimate discussion and smiles and enjoyment with God. Unfortunately, we often make it difficult. We are the ones that have pushed it into the difficult. Often, we substitute the busy for the simple, the program for the personal place of intimacy with our Creator. Maybe we are no longer looking for the smiles, because somehow we are convinced God quit smiling when Adam fell. For some reason, I am pretty sure He still smiles and enjoys it. I think if He had given up on smiling, He would have sent Jesus into the world to condemn it, not to save it.

What a thought, right? The idea that Jesus came to condemn the world, which is exactly what He stated He did not do. Then, why do we believe that was his mission? In the process, we have so easily forgotten our own mission. As long as we believe Jesus came to condemn the world, we will want that to grow in us as a reflection of Him.

"For God did not send his Son into the world to condemn the world, but to save the world through him" (John 3:17).

We lost the fun by believing the switch. We've focused on condemnation. We not only focused on condemning the world with this switch of truth, we condemned ourselves. We condemned ourselves to a loveless, joyless life that has lacked peace and prosperity. There has not been any fun for the longest time. Let alone an attitude of seeing things as adventurous. We changed everything by getting that verse all mixed up.

It is time for a change. It's time to find a different paradigm. It's time to find a different way of looking at life. It's time to be embraced by all of the life of God so we can go back to giggling. This walk with God is going to be an amazing life. We'll pick up what we can as we go. He will leave us so many treasures along the way, we will find ourselves with constant smiles. Yes, this is so fun.

Begin to think differently. Don't for a moment allow doubt to creep in. Address your old way of thinking. If you change, you will find something different along the way. You will find the place of grace that you long for but don't know how to get to. Grace opens wide the door bids us to come and drink from different waters than we have drunk from before. Grace says there is so much more to this marvelous life you have been given than to live in religious servitude to a God that does not require it.

Grace can be a best friend. It allows us to live in this world of fun and immense awareness of the moments where God comes in and delights us with His very tangible artistry. No longer do we need to place ourselves within the shackles of our own driven desires towards a God of our own making. How does He do this? By showing us who He *really is*, not who we think He is. Who He is shows up to be fun, and sometimes we even see that in the moment instead of seeing it hindsight when the moment is gone.

Chapter 37 He Changes Us from Glory to Glory

Believe it or not, when God puts His finger on something He wants to change in me, I think that is fun. I am in the process of learning to live with an adventurous mindset. I want to know my blind spots and I want to change. The thing I like knowing best about this process is He *doesn't* say, "And, oh by the way, fix this," as He walks out the door leaving me without help. I'm often the one that thinks He has moved out of my office like a bad boss. Instead, He says, "Let's work on this together and I'll probably do most the work, if you will let me. You know you will always have a choice." Don't you love that? There is so much involvement from a King who runs the universe and created you. He can't wait to be involved. Too often, unfortunately, I sweat and attempt to change myself thinking if I can only get it right all will be well and I will be a shining light for Jesus. I fool myself thinking I am on my own.

I find the more I grow in this fun faith, I am more and more dependent on Him. My dependency doesn't mean I am weak. It actually makes me strong. I love Paul's answer from the Lord on this one:

"and then He told me, My grace is enough; it's all you need. My strength comes into its own in your weakness. Once I heard that, I was glad to let it happen. I quit focusing on the handicap and began appreciating the gift. It was a case of Christ's strength moving in on my weakness" (2 Corinthians 12:9, The Message).

Isn't that delightful? I had to stop and savor it even as I read it again. I could not miss the opportunity to once again taste and see that He is good. Better than ice cream or Italian food (even pizza). Yet, for so many of us it is easier to replace Him with food or work or a number of things that keep us busy.

Going back to what Paul said, we focus on the wrong thing. We focus on how hard we have to work to overcome than focus on the One who overcomes and gives us the victory.

Having fun is more creative as well. We may have to draw from a different well to have fun, which may be uncomfortable as we dig this well. That is okay. It is to be expected. Fun is very enticing, none the less.

Some don't know how to expect from their brain to think fun thoughts. It was a process. Ultimately, I had to decide to think fun thoughts. You have to decide you will choose to think differently. I have watched the movie *Hook* about fifty times. One of my favorite subject lines in the movie is trying to get Peter to think his happy thought. Everyone knows that until he thinks his happy thought he will not fly. I believe we will not fly in the way we want to until we learn that all of this relationship is fun. Even when it is difficult for a moment, when we move past the moment and we reap the reward, we know it is fun and we fly.

So, the first part of expecting fun thoughts is to ask Holy Spirit for help. I believe I can move past my own negativity into the place of fun. It's deciding that I no longer have to weigh myself down with shame, unforgiveness, fear or whatever keeps me from enjoying this magnificent life God has given me. The same goes for you. This life is a gift. You were bought so you could live in this amazing gift as a victor. It's time we all throw ourselves into the victor's ring, hold our hands up and say, "Yes, I'm a victor. I'm the winner because Christ has made me the winner. He won the war and has given me the spoils." Allow yourself to reach for this amazing freedom of no longer having to work to be a Christian. You are a Christian, not because you work. You're a Christian because you have accepted that Christ died for you and you have invited Him in to live in you. No Worries!

CHAPTER 38 DECISION POINT

We have decision points. That is what I like to call them. They are points in time where we have to make a decision to do things the same old way or move in the direction we say we want to move in. I find decision points fascinating, even though I may stay in them much longer than necessary. I find that staying in them tends to produce my own uncomfortable moments. I have learned to watch myself, almost as an outsider, as I stay in these decision points. I wonder how long I want to stay in them. I kind of smile at myself as I do my song and dance around whether or not I will accept the change God is offering me.

When the decision point arrives and I am at my strongest, I can make a sudden resolution. As if I believed something ugly and unwanted was waiting for me on the new side, my fears are allayed when I walk through that open door and see the beauty of the moment. Thinking I was doing this alone, my indecisiveness had actually dimmed the hallway of transition. In that moment of decision with the door wide open, I walk through and the relief of leaving the past season comes upon me. I move into the place of fresh air and new season.

Every moment has some type of decision point attached to it. The decision points we adhere to when we step into new places are the ones that will produce the results our hearts cry for. Paying attention to what He has put in our heart and saying yes to it with passion is important to addressing the decision points. The decisions ahead are already made with His help.

"But we all, with unveiled face, beholding as in a mirror the glory of the Lord, are being transformed into the same image from glory to glory, just as by the Spirit of the Lord" (2 Corinthians 3:18, NKJV).

We aren't just learning about Him. We are being transformed into the same image. Paul talked about it in Romans.

"For whom He foreknew, He also predestined to be conformed to the image of His Son, that He might be the firstborn among many brethren" (Romans 8:29, NKJV).

We are being made into the image of Christ. This is being done more by supernatural means than by means of the mind, although the mind being on board is most effective as we do have a choice. To go back to the passage where Jesus is talking to Nicodemus:

"Jesus answered and said to him, "Most assuredly, I say to you, unless one is born again, he cannot see the kingdom of God" (John 3:3, NKJV).

Being born again made it possible not only to be saved from hell but to live a different life than we had ever imagined we could live. It's the idea that we can live the transformed life where we are not made into a law abiding person, but changed from glory to glory into the image of Christ, which is what the world so desperately wants.

CHAPTER 39 A WORLD OF FUN

As I sit within all these thoughts of fun, I see the Body of Christ at a crossroads. It's a decision point, really. It asks the question, "What part of Christ will the rest of the world be attracted to in the future?"

"The church, you see, is not peripheral to the world; the world is peripheral to the church. The church is Christ's body, in which He speaks and acts, by which He fills everything with his presence" (Ephesians 1:23, The Message).

You see, the church is to be the influencer of the world, not the other way around. We are to be the ones filled with hope and joy, showing who Christ really is.

Imagine with me for one moment what the world would be like if it grasped the idea of God being fun and ran with it. Imagine how the world, which we are called to influence, would see us. Imagine how contagious it would be in a group, at work, at school, wherever. Imagine that way of life, of connecting, of fun relationships where we are excusing ourselves for our shortcomings and living a life so filled with delight those who know us cannot help but be drawn to what we have and demand they be let in on the secret too.

Think again what your life would be like, what you would be giving to yourself, your spouse, your children, your neighborhood and your city. Maybe even your country. Imagine and allow God to bring your imagination up to speed on this one. Then allow Him to multiply it. Imagine you are watching your world, your relationship with God being transformed into one that brings a continuous smile to your face in the simplest of moments. Then, think again and realize you can't imagine big enough because this kind of world brings possibilities beyond your wildest dreams.

It's time to grab the adventure. It's time to get on God's love boat because it's time for a new adventure. It's something He has always planned and it's something you want. Know that it's okay to be at peace with this because you have asked and it's coming your way.

I was in Dubai on the metro during a time of day when it was very full. There were people from primarily Islamic nations there, as well as people from India and Russia. In the midst of it all, a nudge from Holy Spirit came across my mind. I'm sure excitement filled my face. I realized most likely no one in that car or maybe on that train knew Christ. I was elated, in that moment, as I prayed for the release of Holy Spirit in those people's lives. It was a highlight of that trip. Many Christians might choose to be bored with it. I found it exciting and invigorating. I kept thinking what an honor it was to pray. I carried that attitude with me to Thailand as well. I realized I could get on a mode of transportation and quietly pray for those inside. It was agreeing with God's heart of love for those on the train in that moment.

Agreeing with God in any moment is fun. He sets before us an assignment. It's like mission possible and we get to see ourselves do it because He is big enough to boost us up so we can see it and then we let Him do it through us. It's really all Him. We just get to participate. Then, we get to rejoice in the results.

I love that Father has allowed me to see His heart towards man and His amazing love towards the world. His eyes twinkle with fun. There is a smile in them that releases us to do what we would call the impossible. He continually encourages us to look at what we think we cannot do so He can do it. Now, that is fun.

---

[i] Genesis 5:24

[ii] Joshua's story begins the book of Exodus.

[iii] David's story begins in 1 Kings 16.

[iv] Nehemiah 13:26 sums this up in a single verse. For more information on Solomon, check out 2 Samuel 5 and following.

[v] Galatians 6:7

Contact suzettelambert@hotmail.com

61772737R00076

Made in the USA
Columbia, SC
27 June 2019